# Indelible Memories *of* Yesteryears

## An Autobiographical Memoir

### R. Kent Tipton

Copyright © 2020 R. Kent Tipton
All rights reserved.

# Also by R. Kent Tipton

**A Different Kind of Mom**
(Madrone Books, 1999)

**"In Quotes We Trust"**
(Madrone Books, 2000), Co-authored with wife Lois

**Kid Posse & the Phantom Robber**
(Award Winner, Mayhaven Publishing, 2002)

**Menopausal Mama & Metamucil Man**
(CreateSpace, 2017)

**Pencil Shavings**
(CreateSpace, 2018)

**Kid Posse and the Cave of Death**
(Create Space, 2018)

**South of Trouble:
Industrial-Strength Pastimes of the Fifties**
(CreateSpace, 2018)

**Kid Posse and the Fantastic Ice Blitzer**
(KDP, 2019)

**My Parents: Blanche & Norman**
(KDP, 2019)

**The Journal**
(KDP, 2019)

**Indelible Memories of Yesteryears:
An Autobiographical Memoir**
(KDP, 2020)

**Eight Days of Wistful Journeys**
(KDP, 2020)

**Keystrokes from the Man Cave:
A Collection of Short Stories & Poems**
(KDP, 2021)

# *Foreword*

Dear Reader,

This autobiographical memoir will give you a small insight into the dynamic man that was my husband, trusted friend, sweetheart and companion for 53 years.
I met Kent Tipton at college when I was 18. He was unlike any young man I had ever dated. When I first visited his parents' home and saw his bedroom covered in 3X5 cards with quotations, motivational thoughts, scriptures and even vocabulary words, I knew he was a very special person with depth of character and a clear vision for his purpose in life.
Kent was the perfect mate and husband for me. He was a devoted, faithful, kind, tender, loving, understanding, attentive husband. Kent was honest and a man of complete integrity. Kent had an internal engine that roared in high gear. In retirement he was sometimes referred to as a 'hyperactive senior citizen.' Throughout his life he always had multiple projects in the works, books in the process of being read, ideas brewing in his mind for future creative endeavors, and a list of goals posted on his desk. He was committed to God and his church. He was a true patriot who would choke up when the flag passed by. Kent loved American History and the Founding Fathers. He was proud to be an American.
Kent was an involved, supportive, loving father to his four sons and was always very proud of them. All four of Kent's sons love and adore their Dad in return. Kent backpacked with his sons, coached them in soccer, basketball, baseball, and worked with them as a teacher or leader at church. He fished, camped, hiked, built treehouses, sheds, and kayaks with his sons. He played basketball on the outside court for hours, participated in Boy Scouts and Scout Camps, laughed around the campfire, traveled thousands of miles on vacations, and followed team sports — all to be with his boys.
It is fitting that Jared, his oldest son, has brought this work to life. Jared has art-directed all of the previous covers for Kent's books and has tremendous writing and creative skills. He worked closely with Kent in proofing his books and discussing ideas for story development. After Kent's passing,

Jared found a vast amount of writing in his father's computer and felt committed to publishing the works that were completed but never made it to press. Jared has compiled, edited, organized, art-directed the cover, formatted, proofed and worried over this volume to make it a superb tribute to a superb Father. Thank you, Jared. The entire family is grateful for your talents and efforts in bringing this memoir to press.

                    With love,
                    Lois Tipton

# Part One

# 1

## *Too Good to Forget*

I don't know if it is a sign of a sick mind when a man lives in his past as I often do, but doggone it, I had a very rich childhood and I merely want to hold on to it. I suppose one of the motivations behind my writing is the desire to cling to the past, maintain a firm clasp on a history of happiness. After all, a casual glance at today's world, and one quickly realizes what a mess man has made of it. Inventions and ideas that were intended to catapult mankind forward into a world of mirth, efficiency, and technology, without regret, just didn't do it.

For example, the TV, one of man's most brilliant inventions, has become anything but an efficient tool for mass education. The sleaze and filth that emanate from the boob tube attacking and offending viewers of all ages is staggering. Drugs invented for the management of terrible diseases end up in dirty syringes used to support addicts who were looking for a life of avoidance — avoidance of work, avoidance of responsibilities, avoidance of reality in the here and now. This phony life of drugs ends up costing taxpayers billions of dollars in rehabilitation and crime prevention efforts. Many of the so-called advancements in our society prove to be another barrage on our already beleaguered institution called the family. Professors at universities, scholars with a sacred trust to educate our youth, fill the minds of their learners with anti-family bunk. Free sex is okay, marriage is intended for any two people who consent to it, regardless of innate plumbing, existing laws or morals. The orthodoxy of truth doesn't exist, except in the minds of the tellers of lies who have turned truth on its head. Who gave professors a license to bias the minds of our precious youth? Who appointed them the arbiters of true knowledge? The word "liberal" doesn't begin to describe the bunk these high-paid PhDs spew forth in the name of higher education. A little neutrality in the classroom would be refreshing.

The Internet was another great invention. It's an amazing means of disseminating information, communicating with lightning speed, or shopping for widgets, whangdoodles and doohickies. On-line shopping now accounts for billions of dollars in revenue each year. The flip side is that those who pedal pornography have hijacked the internet for the spreading of their filth, polluting minds, disgracing women and children and splitting families apart. It's a sick disease worse than death. Why? Because pornography hollows out a man's soul and makes of him a walking zombie, totally devoid of virtue, integrity, and goodness with which God first endowed him. Again, a perfect example of one of man's inventions gone awry.

Perhaps with age I am turning a little skeptical of "progress." Certainly, I am cynical of more things now than I was thirty or forty years ago. But my cynicism is an honest outgrowth of comparing today's world with my world of the past, which I will always argue was richer, more innocent and, therefore, better than the world of today. Speaking of that world, indulge me, please, while I mention a few memories which, admittedly, date me, but I am willing to boldly and proudly wear that brand of "old fashioned" as a badge of honor.

I actually remember when . . .

- my Dad's ample garden was plowed by a team of horses instead of a tractor.
- fake butter (Nucoa) was lard-white, and was sold with a packet of dye you mixed into it to give it a yellow hue.
- a quarter (two bits) could buy you something to drink and eat and leave a nickel or more in your pocket.
- we actually showered after P.E. in junior high, and all gym uniforms were ugly.
- the radio played a far more prominent role in dispensing news and entertainment than did the TV.
- you'd never hesitate to pick up a dirty penny. I still don't. Students who saw me do it on campus always shouted, "Scrounge!" I proceeded, totally unaffected by their criticism.
- nearly everyone's mom was at home when the kids came home from school.
- everyone's mom wore nylons that came in two pieces and had seams in the back.
- you pulled into a service station for gas, you received real service. The oil was checked, windshields cleaned, the gas pumped, tires and water checked, and you never had to get out of the car, unless you wanted to stretch your legs or go to the restroom.
- a '39 Ford coupe or a '57 Chevy was everyone's dream car, in which you could do a variety of

activities — cruise Main, peel out, lay rubber, or watch submarine races at the boat harbor, and people actually went steady.
- car keys were rarely lost in the house; they were always left in the ignition, and car doors were never locked.
- lying on my back on a summer day with my friends and saying things like, "That big cloud up there looks like an elephant, see its trunk sticking up that way?"
- childbirth and Santa Claus were accepted on the same level, and I didn't worry whether they were myth, magic, or miracles.
- playing baseball in the street or park without adults was safe, and kids always seemed to survive and have fun. And, we knew a ball from a strike, with few arguments.
- bottles from the store came without safety caps and hermetic seals because no one back then had yet tried to poison a perfect stranger by tampering with factory packaging.
- bottles from the milkman came with cardboard stoppers you could pull out with ease. Even grandma with her arthritic fingers could manage to open the bottle for a glass of milk.
- the corner grocer sold candy cigarettes, tiny wax Coke-shaped bottles with colored sugar water inside, peashooters, and Blackjack and Clove chewing gum.
- soda pop machines dispensed your favorite drink in glass bottles.
- newsreels and cartoons graced the silver screen before the main movie.
- kids chose only between Converse and P.F. Fliers for gym footwear.

- a nerd back then was a kid who wore black Converse gym shoes, wore thick glasses, and carried a slide rule on his belt, or maybe two of the three.
- telephone calls were always at least three-party affairs — you, the friend you were calling, and the operator, who sometimes was your mother's sister, and sometimes listened in, contrary to company policy. Add a neighbor who shared your line and you had a four-party affair.
- you shared your telephone line with a neighbor or two — called party lines. Party-line telephone numbers sounded like this: 283-J or 283-R, or 283-M.
- such things as 45 RPM records, Green Stamps, Hi-Fi's, roller-skate keys, Studebakers, Kaisers, and crystal sets didn't sound like foreign terms.
- metal ice cube trays with pull-up levers were on the cutting edge of kitchen science, then came plastic and the twistable varieties, making the metal ones obsolete.
- all these toys were popular and could be purchased in the large department stores: cork pop guns, dart guns, Tinker Toys, Erector sets, Lincoln Logs, wind-up and friction cars (all made in Japan), yo-yos, tops, pogo sticks and Lionel trains and slinkies.
- you could pay for a movie ticket, buy a bag of popcorn, a Black Cow or Sugar Daddy, and still have pocket change from your half dollar, or four-bits, as we called it then.
- messy mimeograph paper was state of the art in duplicating documents.
- the Fuller Brush man would call on your parents, and demonstrate all his wares from a magical multi-compartment suitcase. Here's your hair

brush, your clothes brush, your handy dish washing brush, and your easy-swipe toilet brush, and here is . . .
- reel to reel tape recorders were the latest craze.
- you could travel twenty or thirty miles in a four-wheeled machine on four-bits worth of gasoline. [Drivers mostly said, "Put in five (meaning five gallons) and not fill 'er up."]. Do the math and you discover that five gallons back then cost about $1.50.
- Bazooka didn't refer to a weapon of war, but to pink bubble gum wrapped in a comic strip.
- you had to shake the pan back and forth across a stove top burner to pop popcorn.
- dentists were just starting to use Novocain to deaden your nerves before drilling.
- you could make a motorcycle out of any bike with playing cards and clothespins.
- stomping on cans so they clamped to your shoes and then tromping noisily about was great entertainment.
- decisions among friends were made by saying "eeny-meeny-miney-moe."
- it was not unusual or weird to have three or four best friends, maybe even eight.
- the worst thing you could catch from the opposite sex was "cooties."
- the biggest financial scam was that somebody used IOUs in a game of Finance, or put two hotels on Boardwalk in Monopoly.
- "race issues" related to whose legs and feet were faster, and that's all.
- "Ollie-ollie-oxen-all-in-free made perfect sense.
- taking drugs meant chewing Aspergum or popping orange-flavored chewable aspirin.
- cafes actually had tableside jukeboxes — 5¢ a tune.

- getting high meant walking on a pair of stilts or climbing your favorite tree.
- the ultimate weapon among kids was a water balloon.
- The Lone Ranger, Howdy Doody, Gang Busters, Roy and Dale, Trigger and Buttermilk, The Three Stooges, Laurel and Hardy, The Hardy Boys, Nancy Drew, Tom Mix, The Bowery Boys, Tarzan, The Shadow, The Hit Parade, Lucille Ball, Edgar Bergen and Charlie McCarthy, Let's Pretend, Fibber McGee and Molly, and Amos and Andy were all major entertainment venues of the day.

Honestly, now, with all our so-called progress today, don't you wish, just once, you could slip back in time and savor the entertainment of your youth, and then share it — just the way it was — with the children of today? That's what's missing today and, sadly, will never return — not like it once was. I suppose it's true of any era. If I could give our youth of today anything, it would be to somehow allow them to experience what I did so many dusty years ago. That era is gone and, with it, some valuable building blocks of morality and decency, and honest fun, so lacking today.

Nostalgia, it's just too good to forget.

## 2

## *From the Beginning*

I, Richard Kent Tipton, was born September 20, 1942 in Springville, Utah, to Norman Isaac Tipton and Blanche Prior Tipton. I was the fifth of five children in the family. Dean (Norman Dean), Gary (Gary Prior), Jay (Vernon Jay), and Marjorie all preceded my coming into the world. Dr. George Anderson was the attending physician, and at that time his particular office was located at 335 East 200 South. I assume that mother missed her regular Sunday night activities, as that was the day picked for my arrival. According to Mom, I came precisely at 8:00 p.m.

I was a very active child, always playing hard outside, getting into typical childhood mischief, and causing my dear mother much worry. I attended kindergarten and first grade at the Lincoln Elementary School in Springville.

One incident stands out in my mind as I think back upon "the good ol' days." Apparently, I had been a thorn in Mrs. Frandsen's side the whole day (first grade), and, after she could take no more of my badgering (it was likely my penchant for talking that was getting under her skin), she ordered me to crouch under her desk like a "little cub bear." I remained a cub for about an hour. I didn't mind the cramped position my body was in, but the tremendous teasing I received from my classmates afterward was unbearable. While in the first grade at Lincoln School, I vividly remember that Grant Elementary School was our big rival. We always called the kids that went to Grant names (Grant, Grant, have ants in your pants), and they retorted with the same (Stinkin' Lincoln).

The next year I found myself in the company of faculty members of Grant Elementary. Now, I had ants in my pants. I had a lot of good teachers while there. I remained there from the second grade through the sixth grade, the whole time calling names at those who attended Lincoln. For lack of contact with most of my grade-school teachers, I can only record their surnames. Miss Murphy was my second-grade teacher; Mrs. Gardner, my third-grade teacher and for some strange reason unbeknownst to me, she wanted to give me a double-promotion. Thank goodness, my parents did not concur. Mr. Mason taught me in the fourth grade; Mr. Bean in the fifth; and Mr. LeRoy Erickson and Miss Gates, the sixth.

I broke my left wrist while in the second grade and Kathleen Russell helped me with my writing assignments. I was in charge of the snakes, spiders, and frogs in our class terrarium in third grade. I always enjoyed the spelling bees held in the fourth grade, and an experiment about how *Coca-Cola* rots one's teeth stands out above all else in my fifth year of elementary schooling. I remember Miss Gates' cooking lesson she gave us. She had some new cookware which needed no water. She explained to us how good this was, because cooking with water destroyed all the vitamins. I also recall that it was Miss Gates who taught us tongue exercises, and to this day I can perform tongue gymnastics with little strain. I suppose that Miss Gates must have been quite an impressive person because I recall many things pertaining to that era. I shall never forget the deep impression Miss Gates' fiancé made upon me and my friends when he walked on his hands for us during a recess period — his change and keys in his pockets clanging to the floor.

I continued to be active in junior high school and tried to put some of my energy to good use by playing organized sports. I suppose that throughout my childhood and early manhood, baseball was my favorite sport. I was always playing, whether on an official Little League team or just in someone's back yard. A season never came and went where I didn't participate with a team. First it was Little League, then Pony League, then American Legion. I always played first base with a few exceptions when I pitched or played outfield.

Religiously, some very important events took place in my life. When I was eight years old, I was baptized into The Church of Jesus Christ of Latter-day Saints. This was on October 8, 1950, and Verl Lloyd Ashcraft performed the ordinance. When I was blessed and given a name in the same church by Solan A. Wood (November 1, 1942), my parents chose the name Kent, but in 1950 when I was baptized, my mother wanted a middle name for me. So, instead of inserting the name "Richard" between Kent and Tipton, she placed "Richard" at the beginning, and from 1950 on my official name was Richard Kent Tipton. It changed my whole life, believe me. The following year (February 26, 1951) our family went to the Salt Lake Temple and my parents were sealed to each other and the children were sealed to Mother and Father.

I was always an active church attender. Though I didn't understand my full responsibilities as a youthful Priesthood bearer, I did know that I was supposed to go to all the meetings, perform the tasks asked of me by the local bishopric, and live the commandments of God as I understood them.

In high school, I continued to participate in sports. I was a three-year letterman in baseball, a two-year letterman in basketball, and I was athletic manager to the sophomore football team because I had an injured right knee (Osgood Schlatter disease) which kept me from playing sports that year. I enjoyed high school very much and remember every teacher who ever taught me. I particularly enjoyed Boyd Wilson's Geometry class, and probably learned more from him than any other single instructor. I also enjoyed my junior and senior English classes from Mr. Eli Tippets and Mrs. Gladys Nelson, respectively.

I shall never forget the ghastly pizza Lawrence H. Barney, Lynn J. Whiting and I made when we were seniors. We were having a regular hair cutting session (this time at Lynn's), and we decided to put our clipped hair to good use. We cut a round piece of cardboard and placed strips of cheese on it. Then we added hair (three kinds, if you please), put some ketchup and other sauces on and then placed it in the oven to cook for a few minutes. After we cooked it, we took it to the school the next day and placed it in the showcase so that others might appreciate our work of "art." I can remember Mrs. Nelson's comment upon seeing it. She said, "that is the most repulsive thing I've ever seen."

I graduated in May 1960 at the age of seventeen. In June 1960, I went on active duty for six months, part of the total six-year program I signed up for with the Utah National Guard. Lawrence, Lynn and I signed up in November 1959. Our serial numbers were consecutive.

I started studying at Brigham Young University in February 1961, after returning home from the six-month army training. Upon completion of my first semester at college, I worked during the summer (1961, for Earl Child). In August 1961 (surprise, surprise!), our Guard unit (116th Engineers, Springville) was activated due to the then prevailing Berlin crisis. I spent a little over ten months in Washington at Fort Lewis with the unit, and finally was released in August 1962.

Bishop Verl W. Whiting approached me about accepting a mission call sometime in August of the same year and I told him I wanted to serve a mission. My brother Gary had been home about one year (from his three-year mission to Hong Kong), and sister Marjorie was serving in Australia at the time. I was ordained an Elder in the Church by my father September 30, 1962. He previously had ordained me a Deacon, Teacher, and Priest.

In October I received a mission call from the First Presidency of the Church to serve in the Southern Far East Mission, the same mission Gary served in. I was set apart by Elder Spencer W. Kimball November 14, 1962 and took out my own endowments two days later in the Logan Temple. I departed shortly after that (about the 20th of November) to the mission field.

I traveled with Wade Richards and Brian Schade. President Jay Ambrose Quealy had been Mission President about one month when I arrived. My entire thirty months in the mission field were spent under his leadership. I was quick to learn Chinese (Mandarin) and tried to take advantage of the short time that I had in Taiwan to serve as a missionary for the Lord.

I had a total of fifteen different companions. I was a proselyting, senior companion for only four months of my mission, the remainder of the time I was either a cooperating companion or preoccupied with other work, such as Branch President, Zone Secretary, or Branch Advisor. I was in the office from October 21, 1963 until May 19, 1965, or roughly one-half the time.

I had a lot of rich experiences and met a lot of wonderful Chinese people while in Taiwan.

Upon returning home, I worked for Ralph Child (through Earl Child) in Colorado Springs, Colorado, as a hod carrier with Jan Felix as a fellow laborer and roommate. I resumed my college education in September 1965. I stayed in school every semester (save summer school) thereafter and graduated with two majors (Chinese Language and Asian Studies).

One very important class I took after my mission was Zoology 105. The subject matter wasn't so interesting to me, but I met a very wonderful young woman in that class — Lois Karen Bonham — later to become Lois Karen Bonham Tipton.

We met in October of 1965, just prior to the Christmas vacation. We dated steadily from about January 6, 1966 on, and on April 24, 1967, we became engaged (sort of unofficially because her parents didn't know yet). We were married September 1, 1967, in the Salt Lake Temple by Elder Gordon Bitner Hinckley, an Apostle of the Lord.

—

## Born into an Era of War

These are random historical notes taken mainly from the Springville Herald near the date of my birth — dates of issue are indicated in bold.

## 9/27/42

An ad for Haymond Drug indicates 100 tablets of Bayer aspirin @59c, Mentholatum @ 27c a bottle.

### Headline: BOND CARAVAN IS COMING

"Springville will be 'invaded' this week by a war caravan sponsored by the leaders of the motion picture industry's war activities committee, being sent out to promote the sale of bonds and stamps and to show people the kind of war equipment their money will provide."

### SALVAGE Drive Begins Tuesday — Metal Scrap Drive to be Launched Here Next Week

"Springville citizens are this week bending their efforts in the nation's most urgent need as the National Scrap Harvest gets underway. Continuing until October 15, it is asked that every ounce of scrap metal near homes and on farms be gathered and placed in the Springville scrap pile, from where it will be taken and converted into planes, tanks, guns, and ammunition for the nation's armed forces."

### —Movies —

RIVOLI, Fri/Sat Red Skelton and Ann Sothern in "Maisie Gets Her Man," come watch your neighbor's ribs shake! Also — Latest News and "Our Gang" comedy.

## 9/24/42, Page 9
### BIRTHS
"Mr. and Mrs. Norman Tipton, boy, at Dr. George A. Anderson Hospital Sunday."

"Mr./Mrs. Stanley Roberts (Margaret Larson), girl, at the Payson Hospital."

### 9/17/42
"Boy, to William B. 'Barney' and Marguerite Liddle Dougall, Sept. 9, at their home. The new baby has a sister."

Full page ad: **WAR BOND DAY 9/26 "SCRAP THE JAP WITH SCRAP"**

### —Movies —
Other titles at Rivoli or Ritz: "This Above All" Tyrone Power/Joan Fontaine.

"Ten Gentlemen from Westpoint" with George Montgomery and Maureen O'Hara.

"True to the Army" Judy Canova and Allan Jones.

"Men of Texas" with Robert Stack, Broderick Crawford, Jackie Cooper.

# 3

## High in an Apple Tree

Many years ago someone planted an apple tree in our backyard. My dad, who had a lifelong love affair with the earth's soil, nurtured it. It was always an old tree to me. I never remember it as a sapling, struggling against the elements like so many other trees that grew up on our lot. I never knew the tree's botanical name, only that it was different. It produced small apples with partially red skin and soft, almost pithy, sweet flesh. The apples were larger than crab apples, but much smaller than Jonathan or Red Delicious or Rome Beauties, Dad's favorite three snack apples. The strangest thing of all was that this tree was barren one year, then fertile the next, and the apples always came in June. Dad called them June apples, so to us kids, the tree became known as the June apple tree, and it became one of the timeless geographic markers on our property. It still holds a special memory for me.

In my ample spare time, I used to climb the tree, challenging friends to higher and higher altitudes, but I also enjoyed ground sports. Basketball was one of my favorites, and I started at a very early age. Most kids in the neighborhood had access to an outdoor court, and most of us owned a basketball. Smoot's dirt court, just over the fence from my house, was the most popular outdoor court in the neighborhood, perhaps in the town. The dirt was hard packed like concrete. We even swept it like a patio, brushing off all the tiny rocks that made for an unsure dribble. We played for hours, free and undisturbed — until older kids pushed us off, that is. Smoot's also was the site of a large underground tunnel that the older boys once dug. And it was the site of at least four terrific grass fires, too. I should know. I caused three of them.

One summer day, even after an exhausting session of basketball at Smoot's with my closest neighborhood buddy, Doug, we still had energy to burn. So, up the June apple tree we climbed, always eager to challenge heights. We were fearless, unless, of course, the climbing entailed some sort of work, like picking apples, or pruning a broken limb from a tall tree that a storm had left scraping on our roof. Then, we were deathly scared of heights and had unsure footing. Our fathers coldly rejected our excuses.

We also liked to talk about nothing and everything. Sitting in this old granddaddy of a tree, about nine feet up, I noticed that the post supporting Mom's clotheslines was snug against the tree. Like all who shinnied up the tree, Doug and I used the top of the post as a seat. One of us would sit on it, and the other would sit a bit higher in the fork of two limbs. It didn't take us long to discover that our backsides were wider than that four-inch post. So, right away we devised a remedy. Off to the garage we went. First, we grabbed some nails from one of the tin cans on the bench, a hammer, and then a nice board about the same length as our rumps were wide, and we were in business.

We nailed the board to the top of the post, and Doug initiated it since he had drawn the longer straw moments before. From that day forward, that seat became the most comfortable in the tree, and we'd take turns sitting on that roost. At school, we couldn't remember the score in kick ball from the previous day, and we often ran out of the house forgetting our lunch money or books, but we never forgot whose turn it was to sit on that homemade perch.

As much as we liked climbing, our older sisters liked ground games, like jump rope, hopscotch or swinging on the clotheslines when Mom wasn't looking. Doug's sister Laurel was three years older than we were, and my sister Marjorie was older by two. Far more important than their age was their weight. They were both considerably heavier than we were.

September arrived and my friends and I started second grade at Grant Elementary. All was well with us; life was wonderful, especially up in the apple tree.

"My turn, right?" I asked.

"Lemme see, yes, I believe it is," Doug replied, sort of scratching his head. I climbed into position on the comfortable seat, propped my feet up on a branch and relaxed. My back was to the clotheslines and the opposite post. Doug faced me, feet wedged in a crotch of the tree, looking not nearly as comfortable as I was. There was still plenty of foliage to give us some privacy, but no apples. We began our tree talk about nothing.

In a mere minute or two, we were off in our world of boyish fantasy, talking about important stuff, like how fast airplanes fly, or how big a bomb it would take to wipe out a city block, or the distance of the far away, billowy clouds overhead. I heard noise in the background, voices I thought. I turned to check what it was. Below us our two sisters were giggling and talking about girl stuff, which was of no interest to us. Second-grade boys don't give a rip about what girls think, say or do, especially if the girls happen to be their sisters. Oblivious of the girls, we chatted on.

We were happy as two bear cubs in fresh honey, doing what we did best — loafing. We always worked hard at it, always. (In truth, it was productive loafing — a pastime perhaps we invented — because during such informal chats, which took place everywhere we went, we answered many global questions, a few local ones, and planned how to use future loafing time.)

I gave the girls another brief glance. Then I felt movement. That's when I took an even closer look. They were grabbing the clotheslines and swinging back and forth until the pain of gripping the wire lines forced them to let go. They seemed to be trying to best one another's hanging time. First Laurel would stretch the lines taut as a bowstring. Then Marjorie would do the same, then Laurel again, giggling, yelling, hanging and swinging.

It seemed like another mindless girl game to me, and Doug looked just as disgusted with them, so, ignoring them as best we could, we resumed our important discussion of how to make our paddleboats go faster in the ditch out front.

"I think we make the paddle bigger," Doug said.

"No. The easiest way to speed them up is to get stronger rubber bands," I argued.

"I don't think so. Just cut the notch deeper and make the paddle longer."

Actually, we were both right, but we couldn't admit such a thing because then we would have had nothing to argue about, so we continued attacking one another's claims.

All of a sudden, I saw Doug slowly moving away from me. *That's strange*, I thought. *Why is he doing that? The tree is fixed.* Then, came a second thought, *how is he doing that?* I looked with more intensity to verify my first impression. Sure enough, the distance between us was growing — rapidly. Then, all in a tick of a clock, a third, and most frightening thought hit me. *Doug's not moving at all. I'm the one that's moving!* It was a death warning that kept flashing danger in my mind, on-off, on-off, like a bright ambulance light. All I could do was yell. "Y-eee-ow-w-w-e-e-e-e. Ahhhhhh!" Then my mind went blank. I don't even remember hitting the ground, but I did, like a falling boulder, left hand first.

I came to in the arms of my loving mother. I faintly heard a jumble of words spoken by her and another woman. They were talking rapidly back and forth about a doctor, broken arm, hurry up, a car, Mrs. Johnson, calling right away, any car would do, Norman's away at work, Dr. Anderson's office, it's his left wrist, how to get there, come on, hurry. I was dazed, and nothing made much sense to me, but I knew I had been hurt because the pain in my left arm was so terrible. Somehow, we made it to Dr. Anderson's office, less than a half-mile from home. (Later, I learned our good neighbor Esther Johnson transported us.)

The doctor — who spanked my bottom to help me take my first breath in this world — now wanted to put an ether mask over my nose to knock me out. (Years ago, ether — actually, ethyl ether — was widely used by doctors to render their patients unconscious for operations. It was a colorless liquid compound that had a nasty, characteristic odor to it. I don't know all the pros and cons of ether, only that before it conquered its victims, it turned them into raging animals, fighting to avoid the awful smell.) I, too, put up a valiant fight, kicking and flailing about until Mom and others restrained me. Finally, the ether won out. I lay almost lifeless on the table while Dr. Anderson set my wrist. I didn't feel a thing.

"How did this happen?" he inquired, while I was yet under the ether's influence.

I was told much later that Marjorie, with some reluctance, admitted to committing the cardinal sin of swinging on the clotheslines, saying, "I guess the post must have been rotten or something 'cause it fell over pretty easy."

As it turned out, the whole truth was that both Marjorie **and** Laurel were swinging on the lines at the same time.

Sadly, that was the end of our comfortable conversation chair in our old apple tree. But there would be better perches in other trees later on. Much better.

I soon discovered that having a broken arm wasn't all bad, even though, as a lefty, it was my main arm. A little later on at school, I found out the truth of that old saying that every stormy cloud has a silver lining.

"Today is the day for our weekly spelling test," Miss Murphy announced one Friday morning. "Clear your desks of everything but a sharp pencil," she continued. "I'm passing out papers now. Remember to use your best handwriting."

My classmates scrambled to sharpen pencils. Everyone except me. I just sat there with a 'poor-me' look on my face, writing hand encased in a firm cast of plaster of Paris.

Waving my cast in the air, I spoke. "Hey, what am I supposed to do? I can't write with this cast on, and I don't think I can do much but scribble with my right hand."

Somewhat sympathetically, Miss Murphy replied, "Well, put the pencil in your 'good' hand and try as best you can." I thought, *well, if you say so.* Then she began to dictate the words. Constantly asking her to slow down between words, I did my best to form letters on my paper with a hand that had received no training whatsoever in the art of handwriting. Of the fifteen words dictated, Karen B., who corrected my paper, said she could decipher only two of them, and that was with Kathleen's help. I got a big F for my right-handed efforts. *And Miss Murphy called that my "good" hand,* I thought.

Miss Murphy knew I could spell better than that, and she also knew that a wrong-handed test wasn't fair. In my mind, it was like asking a baseball player to steal second with hobbles on his feet. Or, better yet, like asking a left-handed pitcher to pitch a game right-handed. I talked with her afterwards as best I could and, of course, being only seven I had no fancy words on my tongue to explain my plight. I just said, "I don't think it's fair that I took the spelling test with my other hand. It's no good at writing or anything else. It's my dumb hand." And then I just looked into her eyes, waiting for a response.

Staring back into my face, she studied me for a few moments. I guess I looked pretty pathetic because she wrinkled her forehead as she listened to me. Extending a perfumed hand, she gently tousled my hair. Then she said, "I agree." In that one short sentence, uttered from the lips of a young, but wise teacher, I gained an immense respect for her because I knew she cared. It was kind of like my dog Jip licking my face. I tried extra hard from that day on to please my second-grade teacher, more than I had ever tried in the past.

The next Friday rolled around and, like any good teacher, Miss Murphy remembered our conversation. She sent Kathleen and me out into the hall to have me take the spelling test in a different way. Kathleen had been thoroughly coached by our teacher in advance. She dictated the words to me, I spelled them back to her orally, and then she wrote them down for me. It was wonderful. I got 100%. Kathleen was one of those straight-A students who never got into a lick of trouble and who always wanted to please her teachers. She was a fantastic student and thoroughly decent person.

I was a boy through and through, and Kathleen knew it. I teased others and yelled at recess and threw rocks at dogs and caused all sorts of commotion at school, and yet she was willing to help me in my time of dire need. That's a friend.

Though I valued her kindness, as a second grader, I never fully appreciated her other assets. She was really cute, her coal-black hair framing her dark, penetrating eyes. Kathleen's warm, ever-present smile radiated good cheer to all. I was later to learn that she grew into a very attractive woman. At the time, however, she was merely another dumb girl. So much for long-term vision.

My cast came in handy in another way, too. Like most seven or eight-year old boys, I did my share of gun slinging — with cap pistols, of course. It was much easier to fire a cap pistol with my right hand than it was to take a spelling test. I used my cast to rapid fire my cap gun by striking the hammer with the hard cast time and time again. Before my great fall out of the June apple tree, I used the palm of my right hand for that chore, but now that I had a rigid cast on my left arm, it was actually easier to cock the hammer. It wasn't long until I had worn away part of the plaster on my cast shooting Indians and bandits rapid-fire.

Time passed and soon my left arm was released from bondage. I'll never forget the putrid odor when the cast was cut away. I'll also never forget how sickly skinny it looked. I feared that it would be that way for life. There were a few red marks running the length of my arm, too, reminders of my persistent scratching with a coat hanger.

Doug and I never rebuilt that simple seat in the tree, primarily because about that time Dad decided to move the clotheslines closer to the garden, and quite a distance from the apple tree, so that he could extend their length.

The clotheslines changed locations, as did a lot of objects on our property, but two things remained constant: the June apple tree, and my urge to climb.

**P.S.** In May of 2000, seventeen months after Mom's passing, we sold the property. It was a sad day, but what made it sadder yet was that one of the first things the new owner did was cut down that old apple tree. I confess, it hurt, and more than just a little. The tree had stood for well over eight decades, and when it fell, a little bit of me fell with it.

# 4

## Christmas 1952

It all started in the summer of my tenth year of life. Every trip to Provo, where the nearest good shopping was located, I caught sight of something I really liked. There, in the window display at Sears, I spied a Lionel electric train chugging endlessly around a figure-8 track. The scene was decorated with miniature trees, train signals, telephone poles, streetlights and buildings of one kind or another. My imagination soared with all sorts of ideas about what I could build around such a train and tracks.

The image of that beautiful train engine with all its varied cars clung to my brain like Velcro throughout that summer and into the season of falling leaves. It became an obsession with me. I still played baseball at the park and in the streets; I still climbed trees and rode my bike throughout the neighborhood; and when school started that September, I went to school and tried to concentrate on what Mr. Mason, my 4th Grade teacher, was talking about. However, in the back of my mind, and too often in the front of my mind as well, that little black Lionel engine, puffing smoke as it labored to pull tender, tanker, boxcar and red caboose, had taken up residency. Round and round it puffed. I was sorely stricken with train fever!

It was around Thanksgiving that I finally devised a plan to acquire that train. The holiday season is when young boys think about the wonders of Christmas. And that's exactly what came to my mind — Santa Claus. I don't think it was more than a few days after Thanksgiving when I first dropped a subtle hint to my mom. I'm sure of the timing because I remember holding a turkey sandwich in my hand while forming the words I wanted to speak. I said, "Mom, I sure would like an electric train for Christmas." That's all I knew about subtlety. She seemed to give no heed to my statement. Perhaps such a request was not in her budget. We didn't have much back then, and after I had said what I did I felt guilty. It must have hurt her to know that such a simple thing as a toy train could not be easily gotten. It was unkind of me I suppose, but little boys have big dreams, and they don't see reality very well.

About a week later we were in Provo again. As we were entering Sears I said, "That's what I'm talking about," pointing to the train. I nudged my mother closer to the window so she could see the appeal of the little Lionel. The scenery had changed to winter, but the train was the same. She looked at the display long enough for the train to make its way about halfway around the track, and then she leaned down and replied softly, "We'll see." I took that response to be progress.

The next three weeks were really agonizing ones for me because my train mania was getting worse. My concentration was shot. I couldn't read with any measurable comprehension, I had trouble talking in complete sentences, and I couldn't even ride my bike with any pleasure. I knew better than to openly talk about the subject with my parents. I knew that Mom knew what I wanted for Christmas, even if Dad didn't, and I was sure that any further mention of it would be taken as whining, and Dad really disliked whiners.

Well, somehow I survived until Christmas Eve, and then I did what I always did on Christmas Eve — I lay awake half the night, checking to see if there was light coming through the windows, then looking at my clock — 2:35, then 3:04, then 3:22. On it went like that until about 4 a.m. That seemed a good time to get up. I sneaked upstairs and woke up my sister. "Hey, Merry Christmas," I whispered in her ear.

"What time is it?" she replied with a sleepy groan.

"About five o'clock," I exaggerated.

"Go back to bed until you see daylight outside," she told me. Somehow, I waited until 6:35, then I was up and ready for the day.

When my sister and I tiptoed into the living room and turned on the Christmas tree lights, I was very shocked. Shocked because there was no train waiting for me. *Wow,* I thought, *I wonder what went wrong?* I was sure Mom understood how badly I wanted that train. I fell into a deep, dark funk. I was so disappointed. *This is the worst Christmas ever,* I thought. Before I sank too low in my self-pity, my mother took me aside and said that the last train in the store was purchased by a lady just ahead of her, and that she ordered one, but it wouldn't be in for another three or four days. That news erased some of my disappointment, but days to me right then seemed like years.

Less than a week later, Mom received a call announcing that her order was in. I could hardly contain myself during the ten-minute ride to the store. Santa came late for me that year, but I learned several lessons. First, life isn't just about getting. Sometimes you have disappointments along the way. The most important lesson I learned was how hard it must have been for my parents to satisfy the wants of their children; not their needs, their wants. I didn't need a train that year. I simply wanted one. I learned later that Mom bought that train "on time," as the old timers used to say. It took her several months to pay it off, $5 here, and $10 there. She was a master at satisfying her children, often against great odds.

My mother showed no stress that Christmas day. She was only apologetic for having disappointed her youngest son. She always put a happy face on everything, and that day was no exception. I wish I had been more understanding of her dilemma, more sensitive to the demands of being a parent and Santa Claus.

In the end, it turned out to be a very memorable Christmas for me, belated though it was. And, I still have that little train — and it still works.

Thank you, Mom and Dad, for your sacrifices, which made all our Christmases bright!

# 5

## Route 454

My parents struggled to raise us kids, I know that – but what I didn't know growing up was how strapped they were for cash. We really did live close to the poverty line, but my mother had an uncanny way of masking all that misfortune from her children. It didn't hurt that she was somewhat of a squirrel, and regularly saved a nickel here and a quarter there, all laid up against a rainy day, and there were more than a few of those days growing up.

Extra money was scarce, even pennies meant a lot. This is why I wanted a paper route in the worst way. I watched the local carriers like a hawk, and they seemed always to have spending money. LeRoy Erickson was one of the regulars. He held the rights to Route 454 in our town like an old miser might clutch his last dime. He was a fine manager of his route. It had been his for over five years. As one of the senior carriers for The Deseret News, LeRoy was nearing retirement, self-elected, of course.

As soon as I heard the news, I approached LeRoy to see if he had any prospective trainees. He was my brother Gary's friend, and this gave me an entrée, slight though it was. He was in high school, and I was in junior high. LeRoy said he had one sub, but he was planning to soon take over a route for a competing newspaper. Therefore, LeRoy said he'd give me a try. I was ecstatic!

Following LeRoy around, I soon learned that Route 454 covered more miles than any other route in town, about 4.5 miles in length. LeRoy merely chuckled at my discovery. Route 454 started on 2nd South and Main with Dr. Otteson, pretty much at the heart of Springville, but extended to the extreme west of town, a half-mile beyond the railroad tracks, hitting a few farmers widely spaced from one another. It also dipped under the overpass on Main Street on the far south of town, and up about a hundred steps that could be traveled only by foot. After the climb, came about a 200-yard jaunt to deliver one paper to Boyd (Bassy) Snow, once our milkman.

As the romance of this potential job faded, I began to wonder if I really wanted a paper route after all, especially Route 454. Then something interesting happened that altered my thinking. I accompanied LeRoy collecting, which was an integral part of the job. I saw the dollar bills and the fat bag of change. That experience convinced me that this was the job for me.

Things went well after that. He trained me. I subbed for him a few times. He found me to be energetic and dependable. I found him to be honest and forgiving, especially when my aim did not equal his. Soon he turned the route over to me, and even gave me his experienced canvas bag, and a few tricks for carrying the super-bulky Sunday editions. Suddenly, I was self-employed.

Generally, I am very much in favor of a young man having a paper route. I'm glad I had that experience. A newspaper boy can learn much about himself and about others by having a route. First, he is an independent contractor. He does a job, collects money for that job, and pays his boss the appropriate percentage. He's responsible for maintaining his bike in good working order, and he's responsible for other supplies like rubber bands, plastic sleeves, and canvas bags. If he can figure out ways to increase his income by increasing his service, then more power to him. Also, he can learn what it means to be responsible. He can't let his customers down, and he can't be sloppy about his schedule. Further, a young man can learn about relations with others, and how to speak to adults in a polite manner. After all, if the customer likes you, he is more willing to pay you when you drop by to collect. Good manners may even garner a tip or two. In sum, it is a maturing process to manage a paper route. You can't be hit-or-miss about your job. When you do it right, you grow. Therefore, I recommend it, but it's all for naught because today there is no such thing as a newspaper boy. With the growth of the internet, print news is a dying enterprise. Most people get their news from the internet or TV, very few from newspapers.

It is worth noting that I had about 52 customers who relied on my bringing them the news from a Salt Lake City publisher. As I recall, the subscription rate was about $3.00 per month, delivered to the customer's doorstep. If I collected the full slate of subscription fees, I would receive about $156. Of that, I gave half, or $78, to my boss, and the rest was mine.

This may appear to be a straightforward business proposition, and from the boss's perspective it likely was. However, my boss didn't have to go door to door and collect the money, quarters and dimes at a time. He didn't suffer when someone moved out and stiffed me out of the $3. Furthermore, my boss didn't have to figure out how to deal with shortages in newspapers.

Also, he didn't have to put up with barking dogs or fussy customers, which were pretty much the same thing. Said another way, my boss always got his full $78, whereas my share was diminished somewhat due to several factors, or hazards, most of which were beyond my control.

The newspaper (***The Deseret News***) was an afternoon daily, except for Sundays, when it became a morning paper. After about one year, the job became routine to me, everything except the early morning edition. Winter was much more challenging because of the darkness of the mornings at five o'clock. As I set the alarm every Saturday night, I said a silent prayer that I would arise on time. Many a Saturday night I had nightmares about my alarm clock not going off Sunday morning. I fretted about not responding to the alarm when and if it did sound. Somehow, I did get up, and got through another Sunday morning. Then it happened.

One frigid January Sunday morning, I slept through my alarm, waking up an hour late around 6 a.m. In a near panic I charged off into the emerging light of day, ugly thoughts coursing my mind. When I arrived at the Fire Station where bundles were dropped off, reality was uglier than my thoughts. I noticed that only my marked route bundle and a few scattered singles on the ground remained. Someone had cut the wire on the common bundle (an unmarked bundle of 20 papers), and other carriers had attacked it like piranhas on a pig. Just like that, I was staring at my greatest nightmare — eighteen papers short, one-third of my customers! "This really stinks," I said to my bicycle, as I scrounged around for more papers.

Since the papers were delivered from Salt Lake City, fifty miles away, what was dropped off at the fire station was final. Once a common bundle was opened, others felt it was their right to snag a few extras. Shortages are a problem in all businesses, but often rain checks can satisfy customers. Not so in the newspaper business. There are no rain checks. Like the sun rising each day, people rely on their local paper for timely news.

As I loaded my bag, I began to mentally select the unfortunate eighteen customers. This was the biggest challenge of my job so far. I went through every customer on my route two or three times, ranking them from nicest to meanest. Then I gave up on that idea. Nice, mean, or indifferent, I decided to deliver the papers in their proper order, and then try to beg forgiveness toward the end of my route from the most understanding customers.

What ensued taught me a great lesson about humanity. I knocked on every door for whom I had no paper. Each time I knocked, my heart raced, not knowing what reception my bad news would evoke. I simply told my story as sincerely as I knew how. For the most part, those I shorted were very sympathetic with my plight. But I had two customers who heaped such verbal abuse on me that I thought I would never recover. One ornery man said, "What kind of a paper boy are you that you can't get up in time to do your job right?" I gave him the only response I could think of. I promised him that it wouldn't happen again, and he said, "It hadn't better, or I'll just quit *The Deseret News*." The two unhappy customers brought up every little complaint they had about me — or the paper, the quality of the editorial section, and even shortcomings of carriers who delivered their paper years and years before my time, which had nothing to do with me.

Excluding the two abusive customers, I had four other customers who expected me to produce a paper at any cost, like I was some magician. To placate them,

I rode downtown and bought papers from the local drug stores. I was able to buy five, and so I also took one to the least abusive of the two irascible cusses. Not even thanking me, he yanked the paper from my cold but resourceful hands. The other ornery cuss went without news that day, and he never forgave me, either. I prayed he would quit the paper, but he never did. I delivered to him until I quit a few years later.

Life's lessons are everywhere to be learned, especially at the bottom of the employment ladder where twelve-year-old boys deliver daily news door to door for a few lousy bucks.

So, you see, delivering newspapers is not all beer and skittles, as the Brits would say. It definitely has its downsides. The weather is always a factor. I have delivered papers in a torrential downpour, and it's not fun. Even before you start out on your daily journey, you must wrap each paper in a protective plastic sleeve to keep it dry. That's time consuming and your pay is not determined by how much time you put in, but by completing the task, every day, 365 days a year.

Snow can be the worst. Not so much when it's falling. There are snow-packed roads during many of the winter days in Springville. One time I was chugging eastward along 700 South, near the end of my route, when my bike suddenly slid out from under me, scattering about a dozen papers across the road. They weren't wrapped because it wasn't snowing at the time, and half of them got pretty wet. I just went on with my route, hoping that I wouldn't hear from any of my customers about having a wet paper. Thankfully, I didn't.

I don't remember ever earning the full $78 in any month I delivered. The world simply is not perfect. There was always some squirrely thing that happened to rob me of 5 or 10%. My parents never made any demands on me to give them any of my earnings. On the other hand, and I am ashamed to admit this, I never offered to give my earnings to the family coffer. Some of my purchases certainly saved my parents a little change, as I did buy needed clothing from time to time. I think they felt that 454 was my baby. I did the work, therefore, I deserved the rewards that went with it. They didn't go door to door collecting for me, and I didn't bug them when I was 18 papers short. I had to wiggle my way out of that bind.

In sum, I learned much about patience; when to speak in defense of myself and when to just move on because argument was useless. I learned about my perseverance, what I was made of, so to speak. I learned that there is a lot of good in the world; and I learned that some people can be genuine jerks, living models of what I didn't want to become when I grew a few more years. Having a paper route is one of the disciplines in the School of Hard Knocks. I'm just glad I got through it.

Such was the life of a boy and Route 454.

# 6

## Of Grease and Pain

It's called Osgood-Schlatter, one of the few medical terms I can pronounce with accuracy, but not without pain. A fair number of youngsters had it when I was growing up. It is osteochondritis, that is, inflammation of bone and cartilage in the knee. It most often occurs in ten-to-fifteen-year-olds, where the yet-undeveloped cartilage of the tibial epiphysis (end) separates from the tibia bone before complete ossification (bone formation) occurs. It usually results from trauma like a single blow to the knee, or a deficient blood supply to that area.

In plain language, there's a piece of cartilage cushioned between the south end of the femur and the north end of the tibia. It laps over the tibia and is supposed to grow to it and become hardened. If trauma to the knee occurs before that thing can completely fuse to the bone, a painful bump can occur, protruding uncomfortably just below the knee cap. That's it, named after Robert B. Osgood (1873-1956) and Carl Schlatter (1864-1934). This condition I will hereafter refer to simply as O.S., which could also appropriately stand for Ouch Syndrome.

Treatment back then was rather debilitating. Doctors slapped a walking cast on your leg for about three months, during which time the fusion of cartilage to bone was supposed to take place. In the meantime, however, all your leg muscles atrophy and you come out of the cast with a leg that looked like it belonged to a ninety-year-old woman who hadn't used it since playing hopscotch in Kindergarten.

Today they usually do nothing for it, absolutely nothing, and most youngsters grow right out of it with no permanent harm. I wish they would have had this do-nothing treatment when I needed it. On the other hand, if that were really the case, I wouldn't have had this story to tell.

O.S. attacked me in the late spring of 1957, at the precise moment when Garth Nelson delivered a swift kick with his right Florsheim shoe to my right knee in front of a bank of lockers in the old junior high building. I don't know why he couldn't have slugged me instead. That has troubled me for over sixty years. We were merely engaged in boyish horseplay. Looking back, I would have much preferred a bloody nose, or a bruised arm.

Around the middle of May, Dr. Judd wrapped my right leg in a cast, after he had determined that I indeed had O.S. The cumbersome cast ran from my crotch to about an inch above my anklebone. Thankfully, because of the banana bend of the cast, I was able to walk around. In fact, once I got used to the eight-pound plaster of Paris sleeve on my leg, I could put a little air in my limp and jog — lightly. Actually, it wasn't really a jog. I guess you'd call it a jog-limp, or maybe a jimp. Anyway, I was more mobile than I'm sure Dr. Judd intended for me to be.

As active as I tried to be, it was definitely not fun wearing that cast. It came with numerous annoyances, especially when I tried to sit down. Usually I had to sit in a chair at an angle, other times I had to stand because the fixed chairs were too close together. I garnered some sympathy from friends, but not nearly enough to offset the inconvenience of immobility. I remember vividly that during the annual yearbook signing ritual, many of my friends addressed me as "Peg Leg," a moniker that I'm sure was meant to show friendly affection, but all it did was elevate my ire.

As time passed, I limped or jimped my way through the remainder of the school year, even hobbling across the stage to receive my junior high diploma from our principal, Mr. Hanks, with muffled chuckles of derision in the background. I tried to be deaf to such nonsense but, truth to tell, I would have done the same thing if the cast had been on a leg belonging to one of my friends.

Summer came, and with it came also a modified plan of survival. I wasn't very effective at climbing trees, so I knew cherry picking was out. Bending down to pull weeds (or tie my shoes) was almost impossible, so Dad put a hoe in my hand and asked me to weed the garden standing up, which I did. Mowing our lawn was something I got pretty good at with a gimpy leg. Of course, most domestic chores I learned to do quite well, thanks to a supple back and insistent parents. Mother was thankful for the help, but I didn't share her gratitude. I was far more interested in diversions.

I even attempted to ride my bike, which was not only difficult and uncomfortable, but it nearly brought me serious bodily harm. *Only when I fastened my left foot to the pedal did I make any noticeable progress,* I thought. I soon learned that stopping was a huge challenge. I had to rely on my injured leg to prop me up long enough to untie my left foot. In an emergency, I was ill prepared to maneuver my way out of danger. After a few painful crash-stops, I gave up, put my bike away and returned to limping.

Upon seeing some of my school friends during early summer, their standard question was: "Hey, when are you getting your cast off?" It became my question too. At my mid-July checkup, Dr. Judd answered by tapping an index finger on the August calendar in a square marked with the number 15. "About four more weeks," I said to myself. I had endured eight weeks and knew that I could easily make it for four more.

The last month of bondage proved to be a time of great inventiveness for me. By now the itching was constant and intense. I had devised numerous tools for easing my discomfort. With some dexterity, I could probe a coat hanger, which I had formed into a three-fingered wire hand, almost to my knee. With a little dexterity, I could wiggle it all the way around my leg. There were two reasons why space was created between flesh and cast: 1) my leg had atrophied and 2) the cast had grown soft in spots. Ohhh, the pure joy of that wire hand was more than ecstasy to me!

The flip side to my success in scratching was that when I withdrew the clothes hanger, I also brought up a wretched stench as well. The foul odor, I soon discovered, was contained in tiny balls of dead skin that had attached themselves to the "fingers" of my improvised hand. An absolutely disgusting smell, it was something very similar to ripe belly button scum. (Am I the only one who probes his navel?) It seemed to stick like glue to my fingers, which made it difficult to get rid of. I attacked the stink with baby powder, spray deodorant and all manner of colognes and perfumes that I found on the bathroom shelves. (Lois thinks I should not share these foul details, but the wretched stench is part of the story, and I like to deal in reality.)

Unfortunately, the combination of concoctions which I poured and sprayed down my leg, once mixed with the native stench, created an even raunchier odor. It was so rotten I had to block it out by stuffing rags into the top of my cast, which then tightened the cast and reduced my mobility. I just knew that the foul stink was eating my entire leg. I had morbid visions of Dr. Judd gasping at the puny likeness of my former leg when he removed the cast. I knew it would look more like a withered grape vine than a human limb, and this worried me far more than the villainous stench.

Sure enough, I endured the four remaining weeks of itch and reek, and when Thursday, August 15 rolled around, Mom delivered me to Dr. Judd's office for my two o'clock appointment, my moment of liberation. By then I had successfully scrubbed the residue of stench from my hands with SKAT, a specially formulated soap with grit like a chunk of pumice. My hands were very tender for about three weeks after that treatment, but they smelled wonderful.

When Dr. Judd brought out the saw, I thought it was a carpenter's circular saw and amputation was next. However, he assured me that the blade only vibrated. Within three or four minutes, the cast was off, and I was staring at what used to be a good leg. It was the color of an overripe banana, and much the same shape, with a diameter of an old man's cane. When I spun around to get off the table, I couldn't bend the puny thing. Except for the decreased weight, it felt just like the cast was still in place. I became very concerned about ever getting my leg to bend as it used to. Doctor Judd assured me that it would take only a few weeks of persistent exercise, bending it a few more degrees each day until my full range of motion returned. He said to progress slowly, and all would be fine. I was a reluctant believer and gimpy patient; he was the O.S. specialist.

Mom had returned to work, and so I decided to hoof it home. It wasn't as if I couldn't walk. I had been doing it for three months with the cast on. Surely, I could walk now that the cast was off.

It was a beautiful day marked by a full sun and a cloudless azure sky. The August heat was just as I expected: dry and oppressive. After three blocks of limping progress, I grew rather thirsty. I stopped off at the Dairy Queen and cooled down with a large root beer. Sipping it, I hobbled my way toward home. Reaching Burt and Ted's service station at Center Street, I decided to stop off, rest and chat for a few minutes with my friends. My parents had traded with them for ages and they would become my future employers.

Seeing only the bottom half of Burt's body in the garage, I walked into the vacant bay next to him and began some idle chit-chat. Stretched over the right fender of a late-model Oldsmobile, reaching for the air cleaner, Burt joined in the light conversation. I stepped back and forth, three or four times as I talked, mostly out of teenage habit, always needing to be in motion, but also to exercise my newly freed leg. The metal grease rack was next to me where I was moving back and forth. Pacing to and fro and talking, the time seemed to fly pleasantly by, and the shade from the garage and my root beer drink were refreshing. I was enjoying this rest stop, which was a little less than halfway home.

Suddenly, things seemed so normal in my mind. I was caught up in the moment, passing time with idle chat. No hurry at the moment, no schedule to meet. I was merely on my way home from a doctor's appointment. Without caution, as I seemed to have lost all awareness of my physical limitations, I impulsively stepped up on the rack with my left foot, the one attached to my healthy leg. It was a change of motion for me. I moved from to-and-fro to up-and-down. Down, then back up on the rack, then down again, the stepping motion continued — up, down, up, down.

Then it happened! Like a flashing bolt of angry lightning that cannot be stopped once it begins its course, so it was with that third heedless step, the step that set so many other events into motion.

A single gob of grease had been sitting undisturbed on the rack, left there from a previous oil change. Of all the safe places my left foot could have landed, it did not. Instead, it came down directly on that one greasy spot, and my left foot shot off the rack like a rocket.

In absolute shock, I felt my left leg launch forward, forcing all my weight back on my lame right leg. You can surely guess the rest. Against my will, my right leg began to bend, then it suddenly, and completely, buckled with my full weight bearing down on it. Nightmarish thoughts jabbed at me as my muscles and ligaments stretched under the weight of my body. The pain of that forced bend was awful! I could not stop what grease and gravity had begun. Muscles which hadn't seen that kind of flexion in twelve long weeks — 84 days — were, in a flash, forced to stretch and strain. "O-h-h-h-h-h!" I cried out.

The pain was indescribable. My leg jackknifed, pushing my right heel firmly into my buttock. "Yeeoowwwee!" I again screamed, as my body landed in a heap on the concrete floor. I writhed and twisted in agony. Rolling onto my back, I painfully straightened out my right leg. No one had prepared me for such shock therapy on my leg. No one could have. Zap! In a blink of an eye it was all over. Instant extreme physical therapy!

I yelled out again, seeming to have no more air in my lungs. Burt hurried to the scene and helped me hobble to a chair in his office. I fought back the tears, but I know my eyes were very moist, as was my sweat-drenched forehead. From there he called my mom at work and she came right away to pick me up.

During the ride home, I recounted the painful accident with Mom. Shortly thereafter I became convinced that I would be back in the doctor's office with more than a cast on my leg. I was sure that I had torn every muscle and ligament in my knee and upper leg, and that only surgery would make me right again.

But I was wrong. By the end of that very long day, the excruciating pain I had suffered at the service station had pretty much subsided. But . . .

I didn't try to move my gimpy leg one inch for about a week. In time, when it healed, I came to realize that the twelve-weeks of "treatment" for Osgood-Schlatter was really fairly easy to endure. It was only a slight inconvenience.

However, the miscue on the grease rack that ill-fated August day was pure torture, pain to the maximum degree. I have steered clear of grease racks ever since. So much for my bout with O.S. and a gob of grease.

# 7

## *Honest Labor*

My high school buddy, Don Allman, shouted from three rows over, "Hey, Tip," pointing toward the descending sun, "take a look. You can't even see the end of these dang rows. They must be a mile long."

Looking up to acknowledge Don's comment, I wiped my brow and then said, "Whoa, you're right; you can't see the end, and I know why. It's because of the curvature of the earth's surface."

"Yeah, right," Don laughed mockingly, and then went back to hoeing beets.

Most of my friends and I had had similar close encounters with Mother Earth. We all knew the color of native soil, and what it felt like against our knees and under our fingernails. I don't think any of us were ever ashamed of this fact. Growing up in an agricultural community meant that summer and weekend jobs consisted mostly of working the farms and orchards in search of spending money. There just weren't many jobs available, so if you wanted the freedom that money affords, you hustled up whatever work you could find.

It's impossible to reflect on my own early work experiences without thinking of several that my father shared about his days doing the same thing: trying to earn an honest dollar.

One time my father was working for Tom Averett, the father of the Tom Averett I worked for in my day, thinning beets. The job consisted of thinning a cluster of tender plants down to one so that it would grow healthy and large and not have to vie with the other plants for needed nutrients. In addition to pulling up all the doubles and triples, as they were called, the job also entailed removing weeds.

Mr. Averett told my dad that if he would lead out and set a good pace for the others to follow, he would reward my dad appropriately at the end of the day. My father always was an industrious self-starter, and he really didn't need such incentives to push him. Nonetheless, he accepted the challenge, and began to set a pace that truly pulled the others along. My dad stopped for water only when his mouth was parched to its limit, and at lunch, he took not one second more than the allotted thirty minutes. After lunch, my father kept up the same grueling pace, getting more work from the crew than Mr. Averett likely would have gotten without Dad's challenging lead.

At the end of the day, Mr. Averett, true to his word, gave my dad a little bonus, about a dollar more than the other workers received, to show his gratitude. When my father, somewhat rejoicingly, showed his father what he had earned, he got a real surprise. My Grandpa Isaac Norman Tipton made Dad return the bonus to Mr. Averett, with the explanation, "Norm, you're no better than the other boys." So, my father walked to Mr. Averett's house and did as he had been instructed. While Mr. Averett didn't quite understand, he graciously accepted Dad's explanation and the money, rather than go against my grandpa's wishes.

Later in life, my father explained that he thought this was a small lesson in humility and pride, and Dad seemed completely at peace with that, but I could never understand my grandpa's actions in this incident. Furthermore, I've spent the rest of my life grappling with the psychology involved. And I still don't understand. Maybe my dad needed that lesson. Perhaps Grandpa Tipton was overly stern. One day I'll find out, maybe.

My father was the eldest of seven children, and when his dad died of miner's consumption at the tender age of forty-three (1927), my dad became a contributing breadwinner in his family. Early in his working career he walked about twenty miles with a friend to chase down a lead for a common construction job out Scofield way. When the two of them arrived, they were told that there were no jobs. With heads hanging down, he and his friend were heading for the railroad tracks to return home when the foreman asked them to stay for supper, and said he would think it over some more. Good luck was with my father and his friend that day, as they were hired for **twenty-five cents an hour**. Dad was nineteen at the time.

One of the highest compliments ever paid to my dad was when a good neighbor, actually my buddy Doug Turner's father, said, "You can always tell Norman Tipton's garden hoe without ever looking up to see him holding it. The blade looks like a case knife, worn thin by all the honest experience Norm's given it." Mr. Turner spoke those words to a group of men and boys in a church class. Indirectly, it was also a compliment to our entire family. Dad truly knew the value of honest labor.

Back to my generation. In addition to cutting lawns and pulling millions of weeds, which grew far better and faster than most crops in our area, I worked for local farmers. Blocking and hoeing sugar beets, once a very important cash crop in Central Utah, probably was my main farm job. We were always paid by the row, and some of those rows went on forever, or so it seemed. The common lengths were 40, 60 and 80 rods. Don was right. If you don't think 80 rods is very far, think in terms of feet. Eighty rods are exactly 1,320 feet, or a quarter of a mile. When you've hoed, scraped, crawled and dragged your body along, bent like a pretzel for 1,320 feet, you know you've done something pretty dang spectacular. That performance garnered you 75 cents, for that was the going rate for thinning an eighty-rod row.

If we got sidetracked, as we sometimes did, goofing around balancing our hoes on our chins, or throwing dirt clods at birds, it didn't cost the farmer a dime, because we were paid for production, not for our time. I admit, however, that we did tromp on a few beets while perfecting our hoe-balancing act.

I also earned my stripes in apple and cherry trees, picking fruit. I was never very good at picking cherries, unlike my brother Gary, who was one of the best around. I never could pick more than about eighty pounds on a good day. Gary, on the other hand, could double my best efforts on an average day.

I hoed and picked corn, harvested potatoes, and pitched peas at the viner (a large machine which knocks the peas from their pods with paddles inside a tumbler) in the dark of night. I did better at these jobs. The viner ran around the clock to accommodate the growers' harvesting schedules. Like all crops, when the peas were ready, they were ready. Mother Nature held the master schedule. You harvested when She said to.

To this day, vivid memories of the pea viner in the river bottoms of Spanish Fork, Utah, still play across my mind. The methane gas from the standing silage was so powerful it not only gave off a foul odor you could almost stab with a pitchfork, but it was also very flammable. Any kind of spark could ignite it, much like a silo full of grain.

Even though my job was offloading the peas, I quickly learned there was a right and wrong way to load peas on a wagon. When layered properly, the vines peeled right off. However, when the farmers brought in wagon loads of pea vines stacked in crisscross fashion, a fellow could herniate himself trying to unload the tangled mess with a large pitchfork. When the tangled messes came in, I was sorely tempted to use some cuss words I had picked up over the years. I bit my tongue and heaved with all the energy I could muster.

As a high school student working at the viner, I also remember my former grade school principal and teacher, Mr. Erickson, paying me a kind compliment. He was my boss at the viner. He said I was a very hard worker, and that he would always put in a good word for me if I needed a job. Mark Twain once said, "I can live six months on a good compliment." I've milked that one for years. Thank you, Mr. Erickson. (By the way, Mr. Erickson was the father of LeRoy who turned over Route 454 to me.)

• • • • •

My mother always helped get us up to pick cherries in the summertime. Along with her many other roles, she was also an excellent alarm clock — abrupt, on time, and clamorous. She fixed us a lunch and a lumberjack's breakfast and kissed us good-bye at the door. She didn't have to do any of this, but she did so because she saw this as her duty. She, too, understood the value of honest labor, and she didn't want any of us to miss out on its lessons.

I don't know why they had to pick us up while the sky still glittered with stars. A large two-ton truck would stop at designated corners starting at about 4:20 in the morning. They always hauled us like so much cattle, standing up, shoulder to shoulder, back to belly. No one could recognize anyone else at that hour because we were still half asleep with faces covered to keep out the crisp, morning wind which whipped mercilessly over our heads and through the mass of huddled bodies. Cherry picking was a job with few warm memories. It was all we could do to keep breathing at that hour. I don't know anyone — master pickers and even master liars — that enjoyed the job. But sometimes there were diversions, which adorned an otherwise dull activity.

One morning we stopped on the Mapleton bench for the last group of pickers. Jack Miller was among them. Jack was best known around school for his lack of coordination and his early start on a smoking career. He could never get his hands to flap in harmony with his legs while doing simple jumping jacks, but he could puff cancer sticks with the best of them. There was no tailgate on the truck, only a single chain joining the two sides. As I said, they moved us like cattle to market. As the truck wound its way along the country roads, we swayed left and right with the turns. The old truck labored up a hill and then suddenly took a sharp turn to the right and down.

Everyone shifted with a jerk to the left, and Jack lost his balance and fell out, right under the chain. Those near the back who knew what had happened began to yell, but the truck just kept going. As word spread, some boys began beating on the cab with buckets and lunch pails. The racket soon convinced the driver that something was wrong. He stopped and was told that Jack had fallen out several hundred yards back. The driver turned around to get him. As it turned out, Jack didn't pick cherries that day because he had broken his arm. After we were let out, Jack was returned home.

Soon enough, we were in the cherry trees plucking red fruit for two to three cents a pound, with the stems on. Picking without stems was far faster, but it was a big no-no. Nothing would get you fired faster than showing up at the scales with a lug of stemless cherries. Truthfully, it's hard for me to reflect on cherry picking as a job. It had hours like a real job, but the money wasn't there. For some of us, it was more of a social experience.

Early in my cherry-picking career, if that's what it could be called, I remember like it was yesterday the day I met a monster in the tree. My buddy Doug was an eyewitness. So, if you doubt this tale, just look him up. He'll vouch for me.

"Can I use that ladder?" I asked Doug.

"Sure, go ahead, I don't need it anymore."

I braced the orchard ladder with its one wobbly leg, shinnied up about half-way, reached out to pick a ripe clump of cherries, and froze. I was face to face with the ugliest, most ferocious, green monster insect I had ever seen in my life. My heart jumped into my throat. There it was about two inches from my nose, staring at me with large goggle eyes. I just knew it was going to zap me any minute. "Yiiiikes!" I yelled and jumped to the ground, trying to escape from the ugly creature.

"Hey, stop horsing around, Tip, you need to pick, man," Doug said, encouragingly.

"There's a monster green bug up there ready to bite my head off," I replied, shuddering at the thought of the ugly thing. "I'm not going back up there, no way. I'll pick in another tree somewhere or get another job."

"Lemme see this terrible monster," Doug said, somewhat doubtful of my claim.

"Be my guest. Take that elevator right there to the fifth floor, turn left, you can't miss him," I said.

Doug climbed the ladder five rungs, searching the leaves carefully. Then he saw what I had seen and broke into laughter.

"What's so funny?" I asked, somewhat upset at his reaction.

"You, I guess. I can't believe you're such a chicken. It's a friendly praying mantis, stupid," Doug explained.

Somehow his explanation didn't give me very much comfort. I think I picked eight pounds of cherries that day, and half of them were donated by sympathetic friends. Net earnings for the day? At two cents a pound, I made $.16 for my efforts. See what I mean? The praying mantis episode bothered me for several weeks. I couldn't get it out of my mind. Friend or foe, the bug was plain ugly, and I knew it was a carnivore.

By any measure, I was a lousy cherry picker, but the ride to and from the orchard wasn't bad — when accented with diversions. Thinking more deeply about it, I guess the most enjoyable part had to be Mom's tasty sack lunches.

### THE PRAYING MANTIS
From whence arrived the praying mantis?
From outer space or lost Atlantis?
I glimpse the grim, green metal mug
That masks the pseudo-saintly bug,
Orthopterous, also carnivorous,
And faintly whisper, Lord deliver us.
— ***Ogden Nash***

Thank you, Mr. Nash, for your comic genius. Would that others might readily agree with us.

• • • • •

In my tender twenties, I remember making $3.33 an hour as a hod carrier, working for Earl Child in Colorado Springs, Colorado. Actually, Ralph Child, Earl's half-brother, was running the job, and — oh, boy — was he a character.

Ralph loved to do battle with others — inspectors, union bosses, suppliers, anyone. As far as I could figure, he just had a combative and cantankerous disposition. Being the gentleman that he was, Earl never mentioned what a problem Ralph was, but I know deep down inside that Ralph must have driven poor Earl to the brink of insanity at times.

Jan Felix and I worked hard that summer (1965), both at our regular hod carrying duties and at dodging the union boss, whose job it was to ensure that all workers on the site were dues paying members. The wage was my top hourly earnings of my life. Of course, I had several jobs at $1.00 an hour, like pumping gas at a local service station, which I did my share of.

The day that Jan was asked to move the Essex mixer from one building to another is worth noting. He hooked it to a pickup, and then took off like a scalded cat across the bumpy construction site. About halfway to his destination, he hit a pile of debris with one side of the truck and when the mixer that was in tow hit the pile it flipped over, bending the tongue in a quick twist. Ralph saw the whole scene, and came running across the field waving a clenched fist and shouting, "Felix, who the hell do you think you are driving like that, Barney Oldfield?" Running up to the pickup, Ralph again shouted, "Hell, Felix, you think you're Barney Oldfield, or what?" In the course of chewing out Jan he used the name Barney Oldfield at least three more times. I couldn't help hearing Ralph's booming reprimand of my buddy, and I also couldn't help chuckling — quietly, of course — behind a stack of bricks. I did feel for Jan.

After I came on the scene to help, Ralph groused a little more and then left, waving his hands and swearing to himself. As soon as Ralph was out of earshot, Jan turned to me with a very sincere face and asked, "Hey, Tip, who the heck is Barney Oldfield?"

"I have no idea," I said, "but I'll bet he raced mortar mixers for a living." Later we both learned that **Berma Eli Oldfield** was an old time Indy 500 winner. He died just four years after Jan and I were born. We laughed about that episode for quite a while and added the phrase to our own repertoire. It's still in play today.

• • • • •

One of the most painful jobs to dredge up and tell was one that Don Allman and I landed through his brother Monte. Monte was a sheetrocker, and through his connections we found Verlie May, a contractor looking for a couple of eager laborers. It was the summer between our junior and senior years in high school and, as usual, work was scarce. Our job was to stock new houses in a nearby subdivision with sheetrock so that the sheetrockers could hang it on the bare studs. We put so many in each house, according to square footage. There were eight-footers as well as the longer and heavier twelve footers that we were stocking. Both sizes came packaged in pairs, and that's how we carried them, two at a time. It wasn't easy keeping up with Don, who was much stronger than I. One of the hazards with the slippery but heavy gypsum board was pinching. If you weren't careful putting it down, you could easily pinch your foot, your fingers, or both. Don and I really worked up a lather at this job, stocking hundreds of heavy sheets of drywall into about eighteen homes. It was grueling work, and we acquired plenty of blisters and bruises to prove it. After each day's work, our arms ached so badly we could hardly move them, and we would swear to each other that this was our last day on this low-life job. But when morning came, we returned because we had made a commitment — and because we needed the money.

Ten days later, when the job was done, we went to Verlie's place to get paid, as he had instructed us to do. Instead of money, we were given the run around. We kept returning to receive our just rewards but were given a number of excuses. Pretty soon Verlie May moved, just skipped out on us. We never saw that man again. No phone call. No apologies. No forwarding address. No rumors of his whereabouts. **And no pay!**

To this day Verlie May has never paid us. There was honest labor given, but no honest pay received. You can probably imagine all the wonderful adjectives we have since used to describe Verlie May's character. In my opinion, stiffing a teenager is about the most vile thing a person could do.

Okay, I'll make one last, subtle plea to get paid. Sadly, Don passed away in 2011, but I could still use the money.

Hey, Verlie May, you low-down, scum-sucking, flaky, no-account, two-faced, cheating, chicken-livered, morally-bankrupt, cowardly, dishonest, son-of-a-dipwad, shifty schlemiel, you reading this? This is your final notice. Pay up, you rotten bag of phlegm!

There, I feel so much better now and if Don were here, I'll betcha he would too.

*Marjorie (4) & Kent (2)*

*Kent in 5th grade*

*Kent (3) & Marjorie (5)*

*Kent in the 8th grade*

## Player Of the Day

SPRINGVILLE—A fellow with seemingly boundless energies is Kent Tipton, 12-year-old son of Mr. and Mrs. Norman Tipton. Kent is a left-hander and plays infielder on the Utah Service Little League team.

He enjoys all sports but especially baseball and basketball. A guy with an eye for business, he runs a paper route, has several customers for whom he mows lawns, and helps his Dad do the odd jobs around his home and lot.

He also likes to build things, and in his Scout work he particularly likes the phases where using his hands to make or do something is involved.

Two of his favorite pastimes are fishing and hiking. English and spelling and band are his best liked subjects in school. He plays saxophone in the band.

*Norman, nephew Kevin and Kent - 1959*

*Kent with one of his dogs*

*Kent's childhood home in Springville, Utah*

Indelible Memories of Yesteryears

*Kent's senior photo*     *Transitioning on defense*

First row: Billy Neff, Farrell Hutchings, Don Allman, Lynn Hales, Kent Tipton, Lawrence Barney, Gary Fitzgerald, Ronnie Davis.   Second row: LeGrande Boyer, Doug Turner, Lloyd Pehrson, Carl Nielson, Jay Jensen, John Miller, Robert Savage, Michael Gardner.   Third row: Grant Simons, Duane Rowland, Keith Sumsion, Riley Rogers, Grant Roylance, Blake Bird, David Whiting, Jim Sheffield, Michael Davies, Don Holdaway.

*Springville High School Athletic Club*

Indelible Memories of Yesteryears

*Little League*

*High School Varsity Basketball*

First row: Ron Canto, Robert Livingston, Paul Cherrington, Dale Childs, Ted Murray, Steven Sumsion, Don Allman. Second row: Lynn Hales, John Child, Kent Tipton, Bill Decker, Richard Williams, David Russell, Grant Palfreyman, Chuck Thorn, and Coach Joe Martinez.

*S.H.S. Varsity Baseball Team*

# 8

## The Fourth Day of July

Growing up, the Fourth of July meant firecrackers, parades, balloons, hot dogs, watermelon and lots of relatives and friends. We always watched a parade, either in Provo or Springville, and sometimes we went to a rodeo. It was definitely a time for celebration and fun.

As a Boy Scout, I began to think about the meaning of our flag in conjunction with the Fourth of July. Sometimes my troop was called on to raise the flag, and participate in a short flag ceremony. I knew the U.S. flag was unique, for I had seen colored pictures of flags of many nations in the encyclopedia. I guess I felt proud to be an American. I really wasn't sure.

I know I was glad to be born in my neighborhood, and I was awfully glad to have friends to run around with. But the question of whether I was proud to be an American hadn't really occurred to me in such a stark and direct way. I didn't know any other life than that of an American, so understandably, I lacked necessary experience by which to evaluate that question in a proper context.

Of course, I loved my life. There was nothing missing in the life of my youth, nothing that really mattered, that is.

However, I don't ever remember standing on a stage or participating in a community play where I recited lines of patriotism. I probably should have, as I'm sure it would have made a deep impression on me, but somehow that was not part of my experience.

I do remember various teachers talking about the significance of July 4, 1776. I did glean something from school. I learned that George Washington really was the first president, and I learned that Thomas Jefferson primarily drafted the Declaration of Independence. Did I appreciate what that document stood for? No, not in my youth. It was just part of our country's history, and history didn't appeal to me that much.

My first real appreciation for my country and flag and all blessings connected to Americanism was when I first put on an army uniform. Somehow that changed me. I began to feel as though I had taken upon me a sacred trust to protect all citizens against any and all enemies of the state.

When I was given the Military Code of Conduct, and asked to memorize the six articles of it, I began to feel very responsible to my fellow Americans. The First Article is as follows: "I am an American, fighting in the forces which guard my country and our way of life. I am prepared to give my life in their defense."

You read that one article alone and you begin to look at your uniform with a very sober countenance. No matter the branch of service, this Code governs all five of them — Air Force, Army, Marines, Navy, and Coast Guard. Same code; same commitment.

And Article Six brings God into the equation. "I will never forget that I am an American, fighting for freedom, responsible for my actions, and dedicated to the principles which made my country free. I will trust in my God and in the United States of America."

# CODE OF CONDUCT

**I**  I am an American, fighting in the forces which guard my country and our way of life. I am prepared to give my life in their defense.

**II**  I will never surrender of my own free will. If in command I will never surrender the members of my command while they still have the means to resist.

**III**  If I am captured I will continue to resist by all means available. I will make every effort to escape and aid others to escape. I will accept neither parole nor special favors from the enemy.

**IV**  If I become a prisoner of war, I will keep faith with my fellow prisoners. I will give no information or take part in any action which might be harmful to my comrades. If I am senior, I will take command. If not, I will obey the lawful orders of those appointed over me and will back them up in every way.

**V**  When questioned, should I become a prisoner of war, I am required to give name, rank, service number, and date of birth. I will evade answering further questions to the utmost of my ability. I will make no oral or written statements disloyal to my country and its allies or harmful to their cause.

**VI**  I will never forget that I am an American, fighting for freedom, responsible for my actions, and dedicated to the principles which made my country free. I will trust in my God and in the United States of America.

# 9

## A Young Soldier Writes Home

I actually put on olive drab canvas clothes and went off to train for war, believe it or not. It now truly seems like another time and another far away world about which I only dreamed. However, the following 16 letters, which my dear mother saved, attest to the fact that I did indeed answer the call of Uncle Sam. I was a green 17, fresh out of high school. It took me about two months to finally close my letters with any affection. Gosh, it's embarrassing to see how thoughtless I was. Oh, gratitude, where are you hiding? Despite my immature attitude, there are a few instructive tidbits here — a little good with the bad. I was a teenager. Cut me a little slack.

I did another hitch for Uncle Sam in 1961-1962, a year at Ft. Lewis, Washington, but I have no letters from that era. Perhaps I'll discover some one day. My entire Guard Unit (the 116th Light Engineering Company) was activated during the Berlin Crisis. We never shipped out to Germany, which was the original intent. We just prepared endlessly at Ft. Lewis.

## June 15, 1960, Fort Ord, CA —

Hi Folks,

Well, I guess I am safe and sound at good ol' scenic Fort Ord. It's Tuesday night right now and I just finished taking a nice, hot shower.

Yesterday we took 12 tests of all sorts; such as arithmetic, mechanical aptitude, verbal, radio code, and so forth.

Today we received all our clothing we need for the coming 5 months & 28 days. We also were interviewed & told our test ratings. Tomorrow we take a medical examination & receive our initial shots.

Everything down here is done "army style" (as you could well guess). One marches to chow, marches to the medical center, marches here, and marches there. One never has time for anything, not even time to go to the latrine. The "high-cogs" roll us out at 5:30 (A.M.) in the morning, work us all day, and then dismiss us at 6:30-7:00 at night. Then they turn the lights out at 9:00. Of course, one can spend the 1-1/2 or 2 hours as he pleases, provided he doesn't go off base, or into any other barracks, or off limits in any way.

I hope you are all well and happy. <u>Please</u> put up with Ruff a little longer. I'll see you in 8 weeks.

Kent T.

P.S. I will write again when I know for certain my permanent address.

## June 24, 1960, Fort Ord, CA —

Dear Family,
This is Thursday night and I haven't heard from you yet. Please write the first chance you get. When you do, send me Wayne Thorpe's address; you can find it on one of the envelopes in the desk downstairs. Also include several stamps in the letter, they are too expensive down here. Tell Dean he doesn't have to send any state beehive patches (like the ones you sewed on my fatigues). We don't have to have them. Please see if you can find my other pair of fatigue pants, (I must have left them home) and send them to me.

It's really a good experience to live in a barracks with 50 other men from different walks of life. There are guys from every state you can imagine: Texas, Oregon, Washington, California, Arizona, Montana, and most of the other western states in our barracks. It's a lot of fun and a lot of hard work.

We get up at 5:30 don't get off at night until about 6:30 or 7:00, then we can do anything we want until 9:00. Lights go out in the barracks at 9. We have to shower every night, perform other toiletries and make our bunks in the morning. There isn't much time for anything.

We started a new class called P.T. Monday, physical training. It is just plain hard exercise for an hour a day.

The sergeants are lousy in number down here. They are just like tyrants. Always yelling at somebody sometime. The food is real good and I eat real regular. I like it down here with the exception of all the double-timing and sergeants' orders. You can't turn your head while standing or marching. You can't go off post. You have to march to chow and stand at "parade rest" in the line.

Excuse the sloppy writing please, I am on my bunk and am in a hurry. Please write.

P.S. Don't forget stamps and Thorpe's address.

Your Son, Richard Tipton

## June 25, 1960, Fort Ord, CA —

Dear Mother,
Just a note to tell you what to send me. I forgot to tell you in the last letter to send me some stamps (4¢ ones preferably) — They cost too much at the Post Exchange here.

I am trying out for the Company "C" softball team tomorrow night and I need my baseball shoes and my first baseman's mitt. Also send me my older baseball hat (high school hat). Not the new one but the other white and red one (there are two of them – send me the older one.) Remember! My mitt without the fingers. It is the newer Rawlings mitt.

I am just fine and happy. We had a footlocker and wall locker inspection this morning; it was bad.

See [you] in 7 weeks.

Son, RKT

P.S. Please rush the above items.

## July 4, 1960, Fort Ord, CA —

Dear Family,
It is about 11:00 A.M right now and I am the only one in the barracks. I don't have any money so I am spending the day on my bunk.

I went to the show last night with Lawrence & Lynn. It was "Chartreuse Caboose." Lynn and Barney went golfing this morning down to the golf course on post. I don't live anywhere near them to speak of. They live in some new barracks that were constructed a few years ago. I live in an old wooden frame barracks. The two barracks are about ½ mile apart. I see L.B. & L.W. every Sunday, usually, (I go to church with them).

It sounds like you are all really "going to town" on the house. I hope you improve it in some way or another. I am glad Marjorie put my name on a gift for Douglas and Marie's wedding. I am writing this letter as I read over Marjorie's & yours, Mother. I will answer your questions you ask me in order that you asked them. (It's easier that way.)

It's hard to believe that Ruff would bite anyone unless they harassed him in some way; but if you say he did, I believe it. Please take care of him and feed him well. (It's twelve o'clock – chow time. I've got to put some boots on to eat.)

Well, I went to chow & to an afternoon movie ("Play or Die"). I had to borrow 25¢ to see the show. I am in debt $1.65, but pay day is Saturday. When I get paid I will send you most of it. I want you to put it in the bank. I will also send my tithing.

In answer to Marjorie's question, "Have you eaten any onions yet?" Yes, I have eaten onions, in fact, they put onions in everything. I never thought I would eat raw eggs, but I was wrong. I have eaten so many runny chickens for breakfast that I can't tell the difference. I have learned to like many things, such as: liver, raw eggs, margarine, raw bacon, and chicken. Lynn & Lawrence have the same meals at their barracks.

I try to get all I can out of the training down here. There is a lot to be had at Fort Ord, if one wants to put some effort forth and really try.

I know all about how Bill backed off an embankment. It happened about a week before I left.
In case you haven't sent my baseball things, don't send them. I've decided not to play.
Take care of Ruff, please.

Kent Tipton

P.S. Send some goodies to me of some sort, cookies, candy, anything. I don't have time to go to the PX. Well, its chow time again (4:30). See you. Write back. I would have written sooner but I didn't have any stationery. Barney lent me some money.

## August 4, 1960, Fort Ord, CA [5th Plt., C-4-1]—

Dear Mother,
I am going to make this very short. If I didn't get killed last week then I never will because we crawled under machine gun fire. It was right above our heads. We crawled at night on our stomachs for 100 yards.

Mother, don't blame yourself for everything. You always rationalize Dad's actions by blaming yourself, don't do it — at least all the time.

About Ruff, please obtain some real good worming agent. Read instructions & follow them. If it says to starve him for 2 meals — do so, unless he is weak and sick to start with. Never worm a weak dog. If he is as weak as you say, then starve him maybe one meal & then worm him good. Feed him a day or so of good meals, starve him the proper amount again & worm him once more. Please don't let him die. I have ordered a muzzle in the mail for him. It should be there within a week. Maybe you can let him off then a little more.

Guess where I am going for my next 4 months? You guessed it — Fort Leonard Wood, Missouri. They call it "Little Korea." It is 100 miles from the nearest town, and it is cold, & very miserable.

For the last week, our company has been on bivouac up in the hills. We pitched our tents & there we stayed for a week. It was filthy, cold, damp, everyone got sick (including me). I am so happy we are back in the barracks. Bivouac helped us all to appreciate these barracks we live in a little more, though. While on bivouac I didn't have any time or stationery to write. I didn't even have any time to sleep.

There were a few parents here for open house, don't feel bad about not coming. It wasn't that important to anyone. I will be home Aug. 13, I think. I received a letter from Marjorie.

See you then.

Love, Kent

P.S. Do as I said about Ruff & he will be all right. If Don Allman comes to take the old Chevy, let him take it.

## August 8, 1960, Fort Ord, CA —

Dear Mom and Dad,

Maybe I shouldn't write and tell you about the activities that go on in basic training. You worry so much about me. The army does all our thinking for us. We don't have to worry about anything except following instructions and obeying orders. They keep telling us not to "sweat the small stuff." They take good care of the trainees here — feed them well, clothe them well, and train them hard. I am sure when I get home I will appreciate home & all the facilities home has to offer much more.

Mother, please worm the dog; I am sure that he needs it. It's too bad the muzzle doesn't fit. Save the address of the company I sent to for it. I will have to exchange it. When I get home I will fix up his pen some. I hate to see him live in such filth.

You haven't told me about Dad working at Thompson; I don't even know where that's at. I hope he holds down a steady job of some kind.

I am only going to take 5 days leave because I am going to start my next cycle at Fort Leonard Wood with Lawrence and Lynn. I want to have someone at Leonard Wood that I know for the next 4 months. I am coming home by bus. I will be home Sunday morning about 11:00. When they wanted $5.00 for a down payment for a plane fare, I didn't have any money. Besides, I wasn't sure at that time when I was going home. I will be leaving the night of the 18th (Thursday) for Missouri.

I am sorry but I can't usher at Lynn's wedding because I won't be there.

I could kick myself for not getting in on the airplane deal. Those guys get to leave Friday night at midnight. I leave at 7:20 Saturday morning.

Well, take care of yourself & don't worry about me. I have never been healthier & I have gained 10-15 lbs. I weigh 165 lbs.

See you the 14th.

Son, Kent Tipton

## August 23, 1960, Fort Leonard Wood, MO [Co. B, 1st Bn., 4th T.R.S. —

Dear Mother,
I thought I had better write a letter worth reading before time got away from me.

Please send me some of those airmail envelopes so I can write to Gary. Speaking of Gary, I met a fellow at church Sunday named Paul Roger Ray (from Arizona) who knew Gary in Hong Kong. Roger has been home for about a year. I think he was drafted into the Army.

These two coming weeks are going to be just as tough as basic; but after that we can leave on pass every weekend.

I am very broke right now ($.45). I don't get paid until Sept. 10th or 12th. I really didn't think I'd need $16.00, but I was wrong. It cost me $6.05 to ride by bus from the airport to the fort. I bought about $5.00 worth of necessary items at the PX, paid Lawrence the $1.00 I owed him, bought some more things at the PX, and now I'm broke. Well, that's life. I would appreciate a couple of dollars (Coke money). I can't even go to a movie.

There are some good fellows down here just like at Ord. Of course, there are those guys that I would consider rotten apples; but one has to expect that.

Please write back and don't forget to start sending my civilian clothes.

Thank you.

Love, Kent

## 3 Sept. '60, Fort Leonard Wood, MO —

Dear Mom,
Leonard Wood isn't any different than Fort Ord in the army life itself; but it differs in the weather, recreation facilities, locale, and that's about it. One must remember, "the army is the army wherever one goes."

I am bunking with a fellow from Jordon, Utah; Lynn & Lloyd Pehrson bunk next to us and Lawrence and Bryan Dunn bunk across from us, and down from Whiting and Pehrson are two guys from Utah, both from P.G. We are all right together.

I am glad to hear Lynn [Hales] & Gayle had a nice wedding. Send me Lynn's address now, will you? (Not his home address.)

I hope you didn't twist your ankle too badly, Mother. Please be careful. I would rather have you leave Ruff in the mountains somewhere than only half take care of him. You don't have the time to take care of a dog; therefore, you are burdened with him. Please try to get rid of him. I am getting very sick and tired of hearing about <u>Ruff</u>!! Every letter there is always something about Ruff in it. Please don't write anything else about him. Just give him away, please.

I received my package the other day and am thankful to have some civilian clothes to wear instead of army suntans. I am wondering why you sent me some pajamas in the middle of the summer when it is 96 degrees and 87% humidity. You could have shipped some shirts in there. Please send shirts that match the socks. (You know, green shirt — green socks, blue shirt — blue sox.) I thought I had made myself quite clear in my letter about that. Everything else was right. Thank you.

I am going to write a letter to Gary tonight as soon as I finish this one. Please take care and try to get along with Dad.

Love & appreciation,

Richard Tipton

Thank Marjorie for her letters and interest for me.

## 15 Sept, 1960, Fort Leonard Wood, MO —

Family,
How is everything at the residence? It seems good to hear from you once again. I haven't yet heard from Gary, I hope I receive a letter within the next week.

I received the other package; everything was just right except you didn't send me sox to match my shirts. Why don't you send me a couple more shirts?

I hope Marjorie gets along in college this semester. Tell her not to quit or get frustrated with her homework. Just tell her to keep working hard & not to loaf. Mother, talk to Mrs. Wilson about my Selective Service before the 20th. I must know what I have to fill out.

Try to get Wayne Thorpe's address up to Utah State University when school starts, will you, please? I finally received a letter from him; but it went to Fort Ord first. He wrote the letter Aug. 6th.

Don't be afraid to send some clothes any time you want.

Take care of yourself, Mother & Dad.

Love, Kent

## Sept. 25, 1960, 1:40 P.M., Fort Leonard Wood, MO [B-1-4, Class 8]

Dear Dad,

It seems real good to hear from you. Thank you for the shirt it is real nice.

I am sorry I forgot Mother's birthday, I am glad I have a sister who remembers things such as that.

Today all of us Utahns are going into Rolla to sacrament meeting. We attended last week and I liked it so we are going back.

There are 6 guys here from Springville in our barracks. They are: Allen Crowley, Lynn Whiting, L. Barney, Lloyd Pehrson, Bryan Dunn and me. We also have 3 more guys from Utah in our barracks: Steven Roden from Draper, Glenn Warnick and Joe Ollivier from P.G.

Gary Fitzgerald and Eldon Lunceford from Springville are in a different class; but are both in our company. So you see Utah is represented well down here in the South.

I hate to miss all the fellows' farewells in our ward. There is a fellow down here in our barracks named George Prior. Maybe he is some of Mother's relation.

I will keep my ears open for any of our relations down here. I have spoken to several guys down here from the South and they said they know several Tiptons in their town.

I am learning about all types of construction equipment and a little bit of how to operate it. We have finished our $2^{nd}$ week phase on the Austin Western grader and the Cat 12 grader. We are now learning about the TD-18 dozer and the Cat D8, Cat D8 series 9A, the Barber-Greene entrenching machine and the

Minneapolis Moline rubber tired tractor. Tomorrow we start operating the TD-18, and Cat D-8 tractors.
It is good to hear from you.
Write back soon.

        Your son . . . Love, Kent

**29th Sept, 60, Fort Leonard Wood, MO**

Dear Mother,
 I am sorry I am tardy in returning your **good** letter. It was indeed an interesting letter.
 Thanks for sending Wayne's address and taking care of my Selective Service for me. It's good to hear that 4th Ward is sending out so many missionaries. I hope Gary gets home in February, that would really be nice.
 Day-after-tomorrow, we are taking off for St. Louis. Our company took 1st place in the parade today (you see, we have to parade every Thursday and compete with all the other companies in the 4th Training Regiment). This means we have no inspection in ranks & no foot and wall locker inspections Saturday. We get to go on pass early Saturday morning. Conference is in St. Louis in the 2nd Ward Chapel. We plan to meet the Rileys this Saturday and maybe they'll ask us for a Sunday dinner at some future date (hope, hope). That isn't the right attitude to take, is it? It sounds like I'm out to get something from somebody. Actually, we would all like to meet the Rileys & talk with them for an afternoon.
 That is nice of Mrs. Wilson to think of us. Richard Wilson gave Lynn Whiting the approximate address of the Rileys, but Lynn forgot it. He was glad to know I had it.

The nights & early mornings down here are really chilly, but the days are pleasant. It rains once in a while down here; but when it rains it really rains. Tell everyone hello & I hope you're all right and happy. Good-bye for now from this end of the U.S.

Love, Son Richard

**6 Oct. '60**

Well Mother,
We went to St. Louis & made it to conference, but we didn't get a chance to contact the Rileys. Maybe we'll try again next week.
I guess I'll have to write a letter to Wayne tonight. I'm glad you got a chance to talk with him. I'm sure he'll like Utah State & I'm also sure he'll get what he sets out to tackle.
Thank you for putting my name on a gift for Birdie. I don't know what I'd do without someone like you to take care of matters such as that at home — thanks again.
If it were my place to advise Keith C. about joining the Air Force & sacrificing a high school diploma, I would never let him do it. It is foolish to just join an armed force, let alone sacrifice a high school diploma for it.
Never mind sending me any more clothes. If I need something I'll write & ask for it.
We had a good time in St. Louis. You wouldn't believe it. As soon as we got out of the car to park at the hotel, 5 or 6 negro boys ran up to us and asked us to buy a shoe shine for a dime. It is a good experience to tour around a big city like St. Louis. I would really

like to go to Europe next summer & do some sightseeing. I just might.
It sounds good to hear from home. Take care. I have got guard duty tonight so I'll say good-bye for now. Write back.
The weather here is freaky — warm days & cold nights.
Tell Marjorie to study hard. I'll see you in Dec.

Love, Richard K.

Enclosed is $40.00. Bank it or save it, please?


**October 15, 1960**

Dear Mother,
I haven't had time to write back, due to the hectic rush & change of quarters. I received a letter from Gary that he wrote when I was in basic at Fort Ord. It was quite old information but I enjoyed hearing from him anyway.
I am glad Marjorie is enjoying school at the "Y." A social life is very important in a school of any type, remember.
I am glad Gary is doing so well in the missionary work in China. He should really have learned some terrific lessons & benefited from living in the conditions he is.
Don't worry about our car. We have had some trouble with it; but we are getting it fixed.
Conference was good, although we did arrive a bit late. We didn't get a chance to meet the Rileys when we were in St Louis, so we will try next week again.
Robert Savage & Larry Rowland are in the same company that we fellows just moved out of. We do see

Ronnie Davis quite a bit. It seems good to have a lot of home staters down here.

Our new company we are in seems pretty good. Lynn, a fellow from P.G. (Glenn Warnick), and I are all together in the same barracks of Co. "C." Lawrence is in an entirely different battalion & so are all the other fellows. We all got split up somewhat, but we still can get together at night & on weekends.

Take care of everything & tell everyone I am feeling fine (except for my back) & living healthfully. See you in Dec.

Love, Kent

**18 Oct. 60**

Dear Mother,

Everything is fine on this end. Just a quick letter to tell you that I have changed addresses again. Please tell Don my new address because I just returned his letter. My new address is: 103$^{rd}$ Eng. Co. (HE), Fort Leonard Wood, Mo.

Take care & please send my athletic jacket & letters to the above address.

Thank you, see you in Dec.

Love, Kent

## November 1st, 1960

Dear Family,
Good to hear from you. Hope you are all well and happy. I am just taking it easy right now in the barracks. I just came in from a hard day at the rock quarry crusher. Tomorrow our whole company goes on bivouac. It is the preliminary practice A.T.T. Our actual A.T.T. starts the 14th and lasts for 5 full days. It ought to be nice. But this pre-A.T.T. lasts until Friday of this week.

There is no class work whatsoever now — it is just working in the field on the end of an "idiot stick" (a shovel); like at the crusher or motor pool. We are supposed to be receiving practical training in the job that has to do with the equipment we learned to operate in B-1-4; but we haven't even been on any of the equipment we were taught about in B-1-4. I have seen plenty of it, but haven't operated any of it.

Why don't you send me some goodies such as cookies, I would appreciate & I am sure some of the other fellows would also. Lynn's mother is continually sending him some sort of goodie.

Mother, you asked me who I would vote for if I were voting in the Presidential race. If I were voting I would probably vote for Nixon. I really don't get enough info about the campaign (or anything else here) to give a just vote; but from what I can gather it seems as though Kennedy is promising the people too much to carry out. Besides I like Nixon's running mate, J. C. Lodge. They have both had experience in world affairs and especially with Nakita and Russia.

Mother, in answer to your question about rug weaving, I would say to try to find a job of less strain. That seems to be a big job to me. I don't want to discourage you, now, but remember that it depends on just how bad you want to do it.

Think it over, & do try to remember that we don't have a gymnasium for a house. Give it some more serious thought and then decide. If you decide to do it — then, by all means do it; but if you do not, then don't keep a lingering thought about it, just forget it. I hope I haven't been too ambiguous in my answer.

Is Dad alright & still working hard?

Tell all hello and be good.

Remember: A happy family is but an earlier heaven.

Love, Kent

## Monday, Nov. 21, 60

Dear Family,
    I'm just sitting here on my bunk waiting for chow to roll around. Good to hear from you. I hope you are all well & happy. Our bivouac went alright — our grade on it was Superior. I had K.P. all during bivouac — real nice.
    I am awaiting my orders to see if & when I leave this place. I hope I leave Dec. 2$^{nd}$ or 3$^{rd}$ — but who knows, it may be the 9$^{th}$ or 10$^{th}$. I think I will probably be home in 10 days but it may be 17.
    I would appreciate it very much if someone would send me that duffel bag downstairs (it has all my bats & balls in it — I think it's in the fruit room). I will need something else to take all my clothes & such in. Please make haste in sending it though.

Tell everyone hello for me – and I'll see you in less than two weeks.

Lawrence, Lynn & I are straightening out the car accident, so don't worry. It obviously wasn't our fault.

Love, Kent

## 10

## Fright Night in Olive Drab

I wasn't particularly nervous when my Platoon Sergeant told me I had guard duty on Saturday night. Neither was I appreciative. I simply accepted it — as I accepted all things in my new home at Ft. Lewis, Washington — as a military necessity. I was eighteen, just trying to discharge my military obligation.

"Be there no later than seventeen-thirty, Tipton," his order still echoed in my mind. I was to guard a common enclosure, a large fenced-in motor pool compound, home to much of the heavy equipment on the base. It also included a military store, a kind of parts house.

When I arrived at the guardhouse at seventeen-thirty (five-thirty to civilians), daylight was fast giving way to a crisp October evening. Already deep grays and brownish yellows were painting the western horizon. The once bright sky was now a soft roof of obscure grays and blues, salted with a few faint stars. A white saucer moon seemed anxious to show its promise as a strong night lantern. Thoughts of past Halloweens nudged one another, brief flashes of bygone days, brought on by the outward signs of the season.

I entered. The Sergeant of the Guard, as sober as a Trappist monk and as nattily dressed as a career captain on inspection day, appeared slightly anxious, pacing the tiny guardhouse waiting for three lowly privates to arrive. "Telford or Tipton?" he barked, staring at his clipboard. There was not a hint of merriment or fellowship in his voice — all business, military style — sharp-angled words.

"Tipton," I answered firmly, followed by a smile. Sarge just looked down at his clipboard again, not even changing expressions. His face looked like it had been chiseled from granite, rugged jaws, sharply cut cheekbones and a squarish shape to its outline. Every speck of his olive drab uniform looked as if it had been painted into place. There wasn't a stray thread or molecule of dust near him. He was almost metallic in appearance, stiff, proper and hygienic.

"Well," Sarge went on, "as soon as Telford shows up, we'll have our three guards, and then I can show you the main object of your evening's attention." I turned and greeted the other private, casually introducing myself. His name was Wilson.

"Since you two soldiers arrived first," Sarge said, "you get the two earlier shifts; get more sleep that way. Telford gets the twenty-two hundred and zero four hundred slots."

Guard duty was always pulled by three men in a twelve-hour stint, two hours on and four off, rotating through the night. During your "off" time, you slept in a guardhouse with your uniform on, boots off, in a small cubby barely big enough to turn around in after exhaling. It was the Sergeant's job to wake up every two hours, poke the next guard to life, and then drive him to his post, and bring back the guard just completing his two-hour shift. At best, it made for a fractured night's rest, but that was the nature of guard duty, and no one escaped its torture, even Sergeants of the Guard.

"Sorry I'm a little late, Sarge" a tall, red-complexioned soldier said, suddenly entering the guardhouse.

"I just hope you're a light sleeper, Telford, so I don't have to pour ice water on you to get you up at twenty-two hundred hours."

"What time is that?" Private Telford had the poor judgment to ask.

"Ten o'clock — p.m., you idiot. Haven't you learned military time yet?"

"Some of it, Sarge. But it doesn't matter 'cause I usually stay up way past ten anyway," Telford replied, obviously unperturbed by the Sergeant's anger.

"Yeah, well, what about at zero four hundred hours, soldier? Will I have to pry you out with a cold crowbar then?" Sarge asked.

"I am a sound sleeper, Sarge," Telford said, "but I'll be ready when you call."

"Well I got news for you, Private Telford. I don't call. I ain't your mother! I poke you with the butt of my rifle. And you either get up pronto or you pull three more nights of guard duty, back to back."

That bit of news seemed to get Telford's attention and erase his oafish grin. I even found it somewhat noteworthy myself as I contemplated three more hideous nights in a dark green matchbox for failing to rise to the nudging of a rifle butt. Private Wilson appeared interested as well, staring intently at the Sergeant's sculpted features.

The three of us piled into the jeep and the Sergeant took off like a New York cabby — suddenly, but not necessarily on course — spraying loose gravel in our wake. I grabbed for the nearest hand brace to keep from flying out. Sarge drove to the northern extremity of the post, an area totally unfamiliar to me. I looked at my watch. It was six o'clock sharp, or as Sarge would have said, eighteen hundred hours.

Gearing down the jeep, Sarge spoke. "This is the south side of our motor pool. I'm gonna take you to the other side where the gate is. You'll notice this area is protected by an eight-foot high, heavy-duty steel mesh barrier. Do you see it?"

"You mean that chain-link fence over there, Sarge?" Telford asked, at the peril of receiving more verbal abuse.

"Telford, I don't know where you're from or how you got in the military with that bovine I.Q. of yours, but we don't call that a fence. Anyway, that eight-foot high, heavy-duty steel mesh barrier is part of the protection. You three are the other part."

"What do we guard?" Private Wilson asked.

"That building right there is the main object. It contains some valuable machine parts, oil of every weight and color, brake and transmission fluids by the drum, threaded steel fasteners, bolts to you, Telford, springs and a ten-year supply of olive drab paint, our favorite color."

Sarge stopped the jeep at the gate, vaulted out and unlocked the huge silver lock, and then drove in. Unexpectedly, he turned to me and asked, "Tipton, what's General Order Number Two?"

I thought a moment and was a little stunned by the Sergeant's bold question. However, having memorized all of my General Orders in basic training, I replied smartly, "To walk my post in a military manner, keeping always on the alert, and observing everything that takes place within sight or hearing, Sergeant."

"Well done, soldier," Sarge replied, not even cracking a smile, "and for that accurate recital of General Order Number Two, you get the first shift. Put on your steel head protector, helmet to you, Telford, and ammo belt, shoulder that rifle, and walk alertly around that military supply structure for two hours. See you at twenty hundred hours!"

With that, he exited the gate, locked it behind him, and scooted away. I was on duty, a prisoner inside a strange compound. I learned well the dimensions of that lone building during the next two hours, measuring it in every way known to man with my two feet. It was a good exercise for me because before I knew it, the familiar jeep was again in front of the gate, and what looked like Private Wilson was getting out. Sarge opened the gate and yelled, "Twenty hundred hours." And just like that, my first shift had ended and Wilson's first shift had begun.

I wasn't used to retiring before nine or ten, but the reality of my next vigil — twelve to two — convinced me to embrace the opportunity while I had it. The next thing I remember was being poked in the ribs with a hard object and hearing the words, "Duty calls, soldier!" It was the voice of Granite Face, faithfully discharging his own duty. His words were like hail pelting me in the face.

Pangs of hunger jabbed at my stomach, reminding me that I had tucked a Big Hunk candy bar inside my duffel bag. I snaked it out and slipped it into my pocket, quickly put my boots on and got into the jeep. The temperature had dropped in four short hours, slapping me in the face like a handful of stiff aftershave, causing my eyes to water.

Arriving at the gate, I noticed the entire area looked like a foreign scene in the thick of night. I looked twice to see if this was the same gate Sarge had brought me to six hours ago. The darkness had truly given the motor pool an unearthly appearance. A strange apprehension gripped me. It was as if I had never been there before. The moon had risen in the southwest and hung bright and orange and full, like a huge Halloween pumpkin overhead. The pine tree that was barely noticeable at dusk, now cast an eerie shadow over one end of the building I was to guard. Trucks and tractors scattered about the compound looked like exotic creatures bedded down for the night. Those dark, ghostly Halloween memories of years gone by came back to me, fresh, vivid and pointed.

Snugging the sling of the rifle on my right shoulder, closer to my neck, I began a counterclockwise orbit around the building, trying to ignore the memories my mind was dredging up. I braced myself against the chilly air and stepped deliberately. My footsteps, try as I might to make them light, still sounded to me like heavy hoofs against a quiet backdrop of night. I pretended I had the feet of an Indian dressed in soft moccasins, but the sound of my footfalls was still loud. I walked on, listening to my faint breathing, peering down at the strip of sidewalk beneath my shiny boots, then at the building and then up at the clear October sky, thinking about military life, particularly midnight guard duty. They were not comforting thoughts, quite the opposite.

At the first corner, I decided to time myself around the building. I was looking for all possible methods to kill time and occupy my mind. I thought ahead to my next rotation in the bunk, and sleep sounded very good to me. Knowing this was my last shift of guard duty was heartening. Looking at my watch I saw that it was 12:05. I had been on duty a mere five minutes. Yet, during those 300 seconds, I had had a hundred thoughts, mostly eerie ones.

Using the second corner as a starting point, I planned my simple strategy. The blind corner I was about to walk into got me to thinking of how easy it would be for someone to hide there in the shadows and jump me. I moved away from the building several yards before turning the corner and did the same with each corner thereafter, just in case I met something — or someone — in the night. On the gate side of the building, the boughs of the pine tree swayed gently in a new breeze, their shadows waltzing on the plate glass window to my left like a ghostly cotillion. I moved past steadily, nervously. *Kind of spooky*, I thought. *No, more than that, extremely spooky.* The remoteness of the site added to my fright.

When I reached my starting point, it was 12:12 exactly. The lap had taken only seven minutes. I decided to slow my pace, stopping if necessary, so that each trip around the building would require ten minutes. I allowed two minutes for each short side, and three for the longs. That way, I reasoned, I would need only 11 more laps to use up my two hours. Also, I figured, the slower I traveled, the fewer scary corners I would encounter. This is how the mind works on lonely, nocturnal guard duty: how do I eat up my time, safely, serenely?

I walked, stopped, looked out across the resting bodies of equipment, which seemed to be touching one another in the night. They remained sleeping beasts to me, perhaps from an Egyptian museum. I recited the words to the second General Order, wondering what the phrase "To walk my post in a military manner" really meant. The thought lasted about two laps, giving rise to several possible answers. Did it mean to use force, like real bullets, of which I had none? Did it mean to challenge an intruder with the sharp point of a bayonet, of which I had, hanging on my belt? What does doing something in a military manner look like?

With about six laps and one hour to go, I fell into a channel of inky thoughts surrounding what I might do if attacked on duty. I tried to shift my thinking to something a little more pleasant but couldn't. Past Halloween memories and the newer dark thoughts were stuck fast in my head. *I know I am locked in here, so running for help is not an option, unless I could spring over an eight-foot high heavy-duty steel mesh barrier. The rifle I am carrying has no bullets in it, and as a weapon of defense is as useless as a toothpick. At best, I have a fancy club. The ammo pouches on my belt are also empty. Yes, I have a bayonet hanging from my belt, but it too has shortcomings. While clean and somewhat pointed, its edge is as dull as a round rock.* My thoughts continued. *What if someone is on the roof right now, watching and counting my deliberate steps around this building? What if he jumped on me? Would I smash him in the mouth with the butt of my rifle? Or would I try to wrestle him to the ground and try to hold him until help came?* My mind continued in this fashion, giving myself a huge case of the frights. *What if he too had a weapon — **with** bullets?* My mind ran away with me, dreadful, ugly thoughts filling my head with every step I took. You think you're courageous? You think you have pluck? Try guard duty in the middle of the night in an unfamiliar, isolated location.

As I paced the long side of the supply house, studying the tall fence (or as Sarge said, "the heavy-duty steel mesh barrier") next to me, and then the pine tree straight ahead, I noticed the moon had risen even higher in the sky. The thought of being alone and perhaps being watched by an unknown presence had seriously fouled up my lap count and my pace, but my wristwatch was still ticking. It was 1:38 a.m. as I approached the corner where I would turn left. I again stepped wide of the corner, just to be safe.

Shifting the heavy rifle to my left shoulder, I turned ... and there before me stood another man! "Oh, my gosh!" I yelled, my heart vaulting into my throat, almost stopping my breathing. I froze, trying to gather my shattered thoughts. As I stared at his shadowy face, I noticed he too was wearing army garb. *Another soldier*, I instantly thought. He was inside the building peering out at me through the window. I heard a loud voice like a clap of thunder, "On guard!" The soldier had his rifle pointing toward me.

I also had my rifle at the ready, aiming it at the strange soldier. We were now staring at each other, a mere six or seven feet apart, locked in a frightful face-off. Trying to scare him away, I made a menacing jab with my M-1 rifle. He did likewise. I moved back a few steps. He did too. I aimed my rifle directly at him, as if I were going to shoot him dead. He aimed his at me. *Maybe he has bullets*, I thought. I began to sweat, even in the cold of that October night. I swiped my forehead with the back of my right hand. He wiped his forehead too. Then it hit me.

I realized I was glimpsing my own reflection in the large window. The bright moon had changed positions just enough to turn the window into a large mirror — sending my own image back at me. The voice I had heard was my own. I felt stupid, dreadfully stupid, but the feeling was far more comfortable than that of fear. My heart was still beating like the wings of a tiny hummingbird.

I spent the remaining twenty minutes of my duty trying to get my breathing and heart rate back to normal. It was not easy. By the time Sarge arrived at two o'clock sharp, I could say my name without stuttering. I almost sprinted to meet him at the gate.

"Get out, Telford, and straighten that helmet!" Sarge yelled. "You're on duty now, private."

As I got into the Jeep, Sarge looked me square in the face, and said, "What's the matter with you, Private Tipton. You look like you've seen a ghost."

I held my useless rifle between my legs and never said a word. Telford waved to me as we bolted away. I didn't even wave back. I reached in my pocket and felt something. *The Big Hunk*, I mused. *Dang! I forgot to eat my Big Hunk.*

# 11

# *My Baldheaded Taiwanese Friend*

I have told this story a few times over the years, but I think it's time to write it for the record. I was prompted to do so by my grandniece, Chelsea Tipton, who served in the Idaho Pocatello Mission. Thank you, Sister Tipton. It's time I formalized this event.

My hair, being straight as brush bristles, was and is beyond training. In my youth, I tried everything from Butch Wax to one of my sister's nylon stockings to train it, but my efforts were in vain. My hair was as obstinate as a wayward child. So, I kept it short, real short, and thus avoided looking like loose straw in a windstorm.

It was September 1962, approximately a month before my missionary farewell and after having had my picture taken for my farewell program. Friends and church brethren descended upon me with the advice that I could not serve the Lord with a buzzed head. Some whispered with diplomacy in my ear, others spoke boldly as though quoting scripture. In sum, "You'll have to grow it out, Kent," was their collective mantra, and I heard it over and over again. A week passed, then another. I did nothing. My hair grew.

I began to feel self-conscious and a little bit guilty about my hair. "Can I truly not serve the Lord with short hair?" I asked myself, and my parents. Their advice was simple: "Just grow it out." So, I let it grow and I let it grow. By the time October 28th rolled around, my hair was definitely at that unmanageable state, about 1" to 1-1/4" in length, and I was now more self-conscious about it than ever. I combed it straight back, or tried to, as a part was not possible. I slicked it down with a gob of Butch Wax and a sturdy comb, but no amount of effort could produce anything that pleased me. Truly, I looked like an angry, blond porcupine with greased quills. However, when the time came I stood before the congregation and did my part, red-faced with embarrassment over my appearance. My obedience did little to salve the emotional turmoil I was experiencing. I'm sure there were more than a few people who were whispering, "Who is the stranger at the pulpit speaking for Kent?" I'm also sure that I was much more bothered by my strange hairdo than the congregation.

With farewell hugs at the airport done, hair poking up against my will, I was off. I landed in Hong Kong, met President and Sister Quealy, bought some new shirts, slacks and shoes, and off to Taiwan I went, still sporting my new 'do. My hair was a constant frustration to me. I did not feel comfortable because I couldn't look my best. Who wants to do anything when they are not groomed right? It was a growing concern (pun intended), which haunted me day and night. What was I to do with this straight straw, which grew longer and longer each day and desperately needed some serious obedience training — training which I knew would be wasted effort, because I had tried everything in my youth. Well, I stood before the mirror each day and tried to make myself presentable so that I could go out with Elder Thayne Green and preach the Gospel to the good folks in Tai Chung. It was futile and discouraging, and even the knowledge that I was doing what I had been advised to do was little comfort to me. I looked and felt like a geek, a dweeb, a real low-life shlepper, but my neckties were really handsome. Maybe people would look at my tie instead of my hair, I earnestly hoped.

Then the news hit around the New Year. Elder Gordon B. Hinckley was coming. He was coming to Taiwan to interview each missionary and evaluate the work in our mission. When he arrived in Tai Chung I was quite nervous. What would he ask me? What would I say? Was hair something I should bother to discuss with a brother of his stature? Would an Assistant to the Twelve want to hear about my hair, or any missionary's hair? I seriously doubted it.

Soon I found myself alone with Elder Hinckley. He was pleasant, humble, and quickly put me at ease with his soft-spoken demeanor. It was the first of a handful of such private encounters I was to have with him. We prayed together; we chatted and laughed together; and as we talked my courage found its way to my mouth. When he said, "Elder Tipton, in closing, is there anything you'd like to ask me or talk about?" I knew that was my opening.

"Elder Hinckley," I said, "I know this may not sound very important, but there is one issue I'd like your advice on."

"And what is that, Elder?" he replied. As best I could, I explained my hair dilemma, how it was consuming my time, causing me embarrassment, affecting my sleep and my work, and then I asked the big question: "Is it possible that you would approve of me getting my hair cut shorter?"

"How short?" he asked.

"I'd say about a half-inch in length," I answered.

Then he looked me squarely in the eyes and asked, "Elder Tipton, would cutting your hair shorter like that make you a better missionary?"

I paused for a moment before I answered. I thought perhaps this was a trick question. Then reaching inside myself for just a little more courage, I honestly answered: "Yes, I believe it would."

"Then, by all means cut it shorter," he said, "but don't make it bald."

Voila! There was my answer. There was my personal dispensation. There was the key that unlocked the door to my happiness. After the interview, I explained to my companion what had taken place, and he said, "Are you sure, Elder Tipton?" And I said, "I am absolutely sure. Come on. Take me to a barbershop." And off we went on our bicycles.

Thereafter, each time Elder Hinckley saw me in the future, he would extend his hand, look at my head and ask, "So, how's my baldheaded Taiwanese friend doing today?" It was in jest, of course, and I took it to be a term of affection, which I have never forgotten.

I loved Elder Hinckley's sense of humor and his down-to-earth personality. He made you feel that he was just another person, just another missionary, but he was far more than that. He was an inspired man of God, who, through tireless labors and much faith, grew the Church in Asia way beyond what the brethren in Salt Lake City ever thought possible.

His accomplishments there were truly amazing. He inspired all who came in contact with him, including the local saints. I was blessed to have served in Taiwan under his gentle, guiding hand.

## 12

## *I Need You, Elder Tipton*

The year was 1964, and the Mormon saints in the Taipei, Taiwan region had gathered for a special District Conference, eager to learn at the feet of Elder Gordon B. Hinckley of the Council of the Twelve, sent on assignment to our area. There was electricity in the air, as the anticipation of this grand event could be felt by everyone. I was there, a young missionary, one year left to serve, loving my field of labor with intense passion, and trying to do what I was called to do — labor with diligence.

Elder Hinckley stood to address the congregation, now stone quiet, but he couldn't begin. Apparently, no one had been assigned to translate for him. There was momentary confusion in the ranks behind the podium. Heads turned this way and that. Mission President Jay Quealy quickly invited President Hu Wei I, one of two brethren who ultimately translated the Book of Mormon into Chinese, to do it. It was a correct choice. He was proficient in English and had flawless Chinese. However, in his humble way, he firmly declined. Perhaps it was the shortness of the notice. Perhaps it was his Oriental upbringing. No matter, the next thing I knew, I was being invited to interpret for Elder Hinckley. Knowing how difficult it is to translate into one's second language, I, too, declined. By this time, I was sure that Elder Hinckley was feeling somewhat rejected — standing alone at the podium, staring down into the expectant eyes of hundreds of Chinese saints, patiently waiting for someone to turn his words into the local language.

President Quealy pressed the issue with me, and essentially told me to get up and do it. I obeyed. I knew when I was outranked. Since I was not expecting such an invitation, I certainly was not prepared for it. However, no one really could be.

Reluctantly, I walked up to the podium and joined Elder Hinckley at his left side. I had translated for new Elders buying a toothbrush or a notebook at local stores, and even for someone giving a Sunday School lesson. But this was a District Conference, and this was an apostle of the Lord waiting to speak. It was not a time for practice, but a solemn occasion for perfection.

The first few sentences of introduction and salutation went smoothly. Then, in only a matter of minutes, Elder Hinckley and I were delivering different speeches, and only his was making sense, but not to the congregation. I was in over my head, and I began to sweat profusely from every pore, but especially from my forehead.

Being the gentle, sensitive person that he is, I could tell that he was troubled. So was I. Upon seeing the beads of perspiration multiply on my head, Elder Hinckley, relying on his rich sense of humor, reached into his pocket and pulled out a fresh linen handkerchief. Then, reaching up with his right hand, he blotted the beads of sweat from my brow. The congregation loved this unrehearsed gesture, responding with a wave of laughter. This only added to my embarrassment. The red in my face deepened and my sweat glands kicked into overdrive. Now I could really feel the moisture oozing from every pore. My tongue seemed to thicken to twice its size.

Seeming to sense that I was still struggling with the task, Elder Hinckley paused, turned to me, and then said, "Elder Tipton, you remind me of a joke I heard not long ago."

I translated, wondering where this new road was going to take us. He continued, "A Japanese woman was surprised one day when she came home and found her husband sitting on the living room floor fishing from a pail." (I translated that fairly well.)

He went on, "She looked at him. He stared back at her. Then she said, 'I'd take you to a psychiatrist, but we really need the fish.' " (I laughed, as did a portion of the audience.)

"Elder Tipton," Elder Hinckley continued, "like that Japanese housewife needed the fish, I really need you right now."

The joke loosened me up a bit, and that, together with Elder Hinckley's attempt to keep it simple allowed me to complete the weighty assignment. Never have I had a more challenging and embarrassing encounter with an apostle of the Lord.

Somehow, I made it through — but I think I did so primarily because Elder Hinckley simplified his presentation a great deal. I don't even remember what he spoke about, or what I said, but I'll never forget the episode that brought us together, side by side, on that stage in Taipei, Taiwan in the spring of 1964.

I don't think I've ever apologized to him for the liberal license I took in translating his talk, but I should. Perhaps the Spirit spoke better Chinese on that day. I sure hope so.

# 13

## *Pure Puffed-Up Pride*

No one wants to tell a story like this in public, especially a returned missionary of the LDS Church. After all, missionaries are supposed to reflect what they preach. They are mirrors of Christ's behavior and teachings, are they not? This is why no one wants to tell a tale whose moral runs so contrary to the Great Example, Jesus Christ of Nazareth.

While serving in the Southern Far East Mission (Taiwan, May of 1962 through November of 1965) I had the following experience.

An Elder Kirby and I were transferred into the city of Tai Chung at the same time. I was the new kid on the block, Kirby the wise old veteran, getting ready to wrap up his term and return to the states. I was not his companion, but we shared the apartment and all that that entails.

One day during Chinese New Year a strange man came to our door with a very large suitcase in his hand. I happened to be downstairs in the kitchen, closest to the door, so I opened it and greeted the man. He asked for a "Mister Kirby," which struck me as unusual, as all of us were known by the title Elder. He explained that he had met Mr. Kirby on a train, was passing through, and since Mr. Kirby had asked him to call on him some time at the man's convenience, he thought it proper to do just that.

I went upstairs to get Elder Kirby and explained that the man had asked for Mister Kirby. Elder Kirby acted a bit annoyed, but he went down and invited the man in. Since the house boy had the mandatory time off during the big celebration, we were fending for ourselves in the kitchen. Elder Kirby had asked the man to come upstairs, where there was space for him to sit and wait. Then Elder Kirby came back down, where the four of us made a little breakfast.

The stranger was left upstairs by himself. That seemed to suit Elder Kirby, who expressed some disappointment that this man had come calling on him. Well, after a while, Elder Kirby went up to check on him. The man said that he was ready to go, bid Kirby farewell and, toting his large suitcase, departed the premises with the courtesy of a Chinese scholar. Kirby breathed a sigh of relief, and we all went about our day.

A few days later Kirby's companion, Elder Winston K. Sam Fong, decided to don his recently purchased suit, one tailored to his broad frame. When he reached into his closet to grab it, he found an empty hanger. Searching the entire closet, he then announced in very strong tones that his new suit was gone! Next, I discovered that one of my nice sweaters was also gone. The four of us did an inventory of clothing and personal effects and found more missing merchandise. I lost a very good camera, two shirts, one sweater and a pair of slacks; Sam Fong lost his new suit and a few shirts; Elder Greene lost a few articles as well. The only one who did not have anything missing was Kirby.

It didn't take us long to figure out that we had been ripped off by Kirby's visitor. The reason for the large suitcase became clear. The guy had easy pickings from our wardrobes and drawers. He just scooped and fled, slick as that.

It was then that the truth behind why Elder Kirby's clothes were untouched became apparent. What he wore was not worth taking. He always looked a little shabby, a little tattered, in fact. He wore neckties that companions returning home had given him, stretched long and narrow from the many hands that had knotted them and pulled them into position. His shirts were very thin, and his slacks were less than neat. He confessed to us that the clothing he had tailored for him in Hong Kong nearly two and one-half years ago remained unworn in his large aluminum trunk. He apparently wanted to save them for use back home.

His confession did not ease Sam Fong's ire, believe me. But then Kirby continued. He had met the man on the train during the transfers. Often an Elder would be placed on a train to his new destination solo. Then he would be met by Elders at the station of his new city. During the conversation with the man, Elder Kirby had fabricated quite a story. He was a student, studying in Taiwan, never mentioned the Church, and gave the man his new address in Tai Chung, our apartment and church building.

We were certain that one con had scammed another, which sort of makes a point, does it not? Instead of humbly being about the Lord's business, he arrogantly concocted a lie. It certainly illustrates the scripture in Proverbs that pride precedes the fall.

*Basic training, Fort Ord, CA, 1960*

*Ft. Lewis, Washington, ~age 18*

*Elder Carlson & Elder Tipton, 1964 - Taiwan*

*Elder Tipton & Elder Carlson – Taiwan*

*August 2, 1964 – Kent translating at a Chapel Groundbreaking Ceremony in Kaohsiung City*

*Attending church in Taiwan*

*Kent with parents & nephew Wesley, 1967*

# Part Two

# 14

## *Why 1, 3, & 7 Are My Favorite Numbers*

It's not why you think. I know, you've already added up my favorite three numbers and think that because they total eleven, and eleven is widely thought to be a lucky number, that this is the reason I like these numbers. Wrong! Dead wrong!

For 25 years my address never changed. It was as constant as the morning sun. All through my childhood and into adulthood I knew only one home, one yard, one front porch, and one address. That constancy gave me stability and comfort, reduced worry, and allowed me to concentrate on more important things. Things like: in which tree should I build a tree house? What game can I next create to fool my dog? Or, which days this week shall I play basketball after school?

You see, I grew up in the best of times and in an ideal place for me. My home address was 137 North 400 East, Springville, Utah. I was a free-spirited country boy, susceptible to the influences of the social forces of the 40s and 50s, and those truly were golden decades.

Without a bunch of electronic devices, kids back then made their own fun. True, life was simpler back then, but it was authentic. Within two or three miles of 137, walking distance really, were many attractions (my parents may have considered them distractions). A state fish hatchery, which was home to all sizes of fish, from minnows to lunkers, was just down a nearby lane, over a fence, and through the cattails. In the opposite direction was Hobble Creek Canyon, a short bike ride uphill, and there I could fish, swim or hike. The beautiful mountains were constantly beckoning to me to explore for hidden caves, or to climb to the summit and fill my lungs with fresh air. To the west lay Utah Lake, an attraction that required a bicycle to enjoy, as it was about eight miles away. There I could swim or fish for catfish in the summer, and hunt ducks or ice skate in the winter. These were only a few of the nearby attractions. There were many others that were great fun as well.

My childhood was rich in tangible, hands-on activities. For example, I never owned a new bicycle until I had been married for about a year. However, as a youngster I assembled a really good bike from discarded parts of five or six bikes that my older brothers tossed in the corner of our old chicken coup. Putting a bike together from odds and ends taught me much about how a bike works, including bearings, brakes, spokes and sprockets. When my "Heinz 57" bike broke down, I either fixed it or I walked. I really hated to walk. I learned how to fix flat tires, adjust handlebars and seats, and repair broken chains or pedals. It was a good experience because in the repairing process I learned much about my dad's tools.

When I daydreamed, I dreamed of being outdoors, playing baseball, inventing, or swinging on a rope swing. Sitting around the house reading a book was my idea of torture. I always felt like nature could teach me much more than books. I was an outside person, period. Thankfully, I had several buddies who thought like I did, and we had a blast exploring, inventing, experimenting, and just plain living big in the great outdoors.

My buddies had stable addresses too. Numbers like 289, 311 and 142 quickly come to mind. They were all within walking distance of 137. When it comes right down to it, I guess these numbers represented the real main attractions, for without my friends, the mountains and the water wouldn't have been very exciting. My friendships made everything else interesting. After all, what good is a tree house without friends with whom to share it? How fun is fishing solo? How could I play competitive basketball without other players?

I don't think you want a complete biography, and I don't feel like writing one. I just wanted to point out why 1, 3, and 7 are my very favorite numbers. I think I've done that. And now you know too.

# 15

## *In Praise of Hugs*

I love hugs. As far back as my memory serves, I have clear and happy images of brothers, sister, aunts and Mother hugging me. I suppose it all started at the moment my mother first took me to her breast in that incomparable mother-child embrace of honest affection. All I know is that the enjoyment of a good hug has never left me. My mother breastfed every one of her five children and, as she did, she poured every bit of her love and joy and passion into that act as if each feeding were a final sacred rite. She knew the binding power of that simple ritual, and she cherished and respected it. Those were my first hugs: in the arms of a nourishing mother. And I became a believer in the power of the tight embrace.

What is a hug, anyway? Lexicons of every variety agree that it is a tight clasp with the arms, a warm embrace. My trusty 1927 edition enters the verb form as:

*"To clasp tightly in the arms with affection; embrace closely or warmly."*

In part, Wikipedia says, *"A hug is a near universal form of physical intimacy, in which two people put their arms around the neck, back, or waist of one another and hold each other closely. If more than two persons are involved, this is referred to as a group hug. A hug, sometimes in association with a kiss, is a form of nonverbal communication. A hug is usually a demonstration of affection and emotional warmth, sometimes arising out of joy or happiness at meeting someone or seeing someone that they have not seen in a long time. A non-reciprocal hug may demonstrate a problem in the relationship. An unexpected hug can be regarded as an invasion of a person's personal space, but if it is reciprocated it is an indication that it is welcome . . . "*

Actually, I don't know anyone so dumb as to not know the meaning of a hug. Even toddlers with fumbling words and unsure tongues can demonstrate it. Down's syndrome David, who frequents the Sonora gym, gets hugs regularly from fellow exercisers. He knows what a hug means. Experts agree that a hug implies affection, that point is important. It is also important to note that there is no one-word synonym for "hug" in our language. Definitions aside, I am far more interested in the why aspect, rather than the what aspect, of hugs.

Why do people hug? That's the kernel of the topic. All else is husk, light and flimsy, to be blown away with a puff of wind. Human beings hug for the same reasons they wave, or sign, or shake hands, or share any other physical exchanges. People wave when they depart or when they arrive. People shake hands when greeting or saying farewell to friends and strangers. They give a thumbs-up sign to friends on similar occasions. People kiss when greeting and parting. And people hug on those occasions as well. Hugging means affection.

When your child scores the winning soccer goal, or overcomes acute fright to deliver a bit part in a play, or his football team wins a close one, parents, players, and onlookers hug in triumph. It is a symbol of accomplishment, and people need recognition. In short, hugs are an expression of appreciation, fondness and, yes, love for others. That's why people hug. People hug people that they like. It plays a significant role in building self-esteem because a hug says to another, "You are worthy of my appreciation, my admiration, my love. I like you." And that's a good thing. The more hugging we have in the world, the better the world is.

The recent Olympic Games give us yet another opportunity to see hugs in action. Coach embraces petite diver. Diver feels accepted, praised; coach knows a hug is worth many sentences of thanks and so he feels good too. Women's basketball players rush to center court and hug each other in a jumping jubilation. They're cheering for each other and telling the world how happy they are. It feels good to hug in victory or defeat. Sprinter hugs loved ones in stands after pouring out his all in a strenuous run to the finish line. It's a mutual thing. He's thanking them for their support, and they are thanking him for his four years of effort in preparation for this biggest of all races. And the beach volleyballers and soccer players and gymnasts and bikers and boxers all hug as well.

But the hug I like the most is the unearned hug from a grandchild who just wants to show some affection for grandpa. Would I turn this offering away? Not on your life. A hug like that is worth more than Olympic gold. I have joyously hugged every one of my grandchildren, and will continue to do so, because those hugs are priceless. They serve to cement a relationship that can be built in no other way. When grandchild and grandfather embrace, the two are saying the same thing at the same time without even uttering a syllable. They are saying, "Hey, you're okay, and I love you very much." Relationships like that require years of hugs to bring to fruition.

In conclusion, we know that people hug and touch to initiate and sustain cooperation. They hug to demonstrate feelings of appreciation and affection. They hug because they want to share their feelings of joy, love and acceptance with others. Huggers are generally happy people. And I want to be one of them.

You know what? I just love hugs.

—

**Note:** For those who want to delve into the scientific and religious aspects of hugs, please read on. The rest of you may turn out the light and go to sleep.

First, I'd like to recommend a book. The author, Paul J. Zak, suggests that touching and hugging may have real health benefits. His new book is titled The Moral Molecule. In it he explores the amino acid molecule oxytocin's effect on behavior. He claims that, "Touch needs to be freely given and accepted to have a positive effect." One study has shown that hugs increase levels of oxytocin and reduce blood pressure. Oxytocin is a mammalian hormone that acts primarily as a neuromodulator in the brain. The ability to secrete this hormone is a good thing.

On the other hand, according to researchers, the inability to secrete oxytocin and feel empathy is linked to sociopathy, psychopathy, narcissism, and general manipulativeness. And this condition is not so good.

Finally, there are many examples of the spiritual power of hugs, but I will cite only one here. President Harold B. Lee's "miracle file" contained letters from people whose lives had been touched by miracles. One young college coed wrote later, "To have an apostle put his arms around you and cradle you like a little child and bless you was like nothing I could imagine. I got a glimpse of Christlike love . . . ." [Modern-Day Miracles by L. Brent Goates, p. 15]

There is much, much more to learn about this wonderful phenomenon called a hug, but both time and space are limited. Dig and delve further on your own.

# 16

## *Freedom*

Freedom itself is not declining. It's the lack of appreciation for it that is in a bear market. I have worked in the public school system in two different states for twenty-five years. In my day to day work I see too much confusion about what blessings this country gives us. I am a die-hard patriot, and I love America. I just wish an end would soon come to the America bashing that is running rampant in our country. Twenty years ago, I do not remember students being so confused about what America stands for. Today, many are uncertain as to whether this is a good place to live, much less being the best country in the world.

Back in November of 1979, shortly after communist China had opened up to outsiders, I had the distinct honor of touring with about 50 others. It was a business trip with Howard Ruff's subscribers. Because of my language ability, I was appointed "Group Leader," a glorified title for baggage checker, translator and hat buyer. But my purpose here is not to retell the entire 15-day trip. It is to speak to the topic of freedom.

We visited five cities and traveled over 2500 miles. We were under the pall of communist oppression for the full 15 days. The heavy political and social ideologies prevalent there could be felt everywhere we went. The schools were regimented, mechanical and very old fashioned. I saw few signs of verve, diverse thinking, or individual creativity. Some of the playground toys were from a military obstacle course.

In the hinterland, including the capital city of Peking, the clothing was drab and depressing. Out in public, as far as the eye could see, solid blues, blacks and greenish tans made up the landscape. I saw no reds or yellows or fancy prints on clothing and no western style dresses until we visited Shanghai.

In the few communes we visited, the people didn't seem to enjoy life at all. I did see a few youngsters smile at us, but the adults had expressions that seemed frozen in agony and despair.

The routes our buses took were all predetermined, our shopping closely monitored. We ate where the guide took us, all by prior arrangement. We all felt inhibited, devitalized, restrained and oppressed.

In everything we did, we seemed to do it under a cloud of suspicion. I was feeling handcuffed most of the time. One day I broke away from the group and went to a few shops by myself. It was exhilarating to say the least.

At first the psychological impact of those silent fetters on us Westerners was not readily noticeable. No one openly talked about it during the tour. However, there was a mood which slowly, steadily, over 15 days, crept upon, around and into each one of us. A feeling of gloom and hopelessness just seemed silently to grow within each traveler. The return leg from Canton to Hong Kong via train was the moment of truth.

All of us were in one car together. At first there was conversation and even friendly card games. The mood was light and cheery. We had no idea, beyond the diner car, what else was on board with us. We just knew that we were returning from communist China to Hong Kong. As time passed, and we drew closer and closer to our destination, the conversations grew softer and fewer. Soon a sign appeared that we were approaching Hong Kong. Everyone drew silent, as if by some command. Not a word was spoken for miles and miles, the anticipation of Hong Kong so strong.

As we crossed the border into Hong Kong the train car erupted with thankful cheers. The freedom we were all used to was not part of our lives for 15 very long days, and now we were celebrating our freedom again. Imagine Hong Kong being thought of as the haven of freedom we all sought.

I think it takes living in another country for at least a few weeks to really appreciate what we have here in this glorious land. As the old saying goes, you never miss the water till the well runs dry, and that is surely true of our freedom in this great country.

# 17

## *Tattoos & Smoking*

My attitude toward tattoos is pretty straightforward: if God had wanted permanent designs on all His children's skin, He would have decorated them in the womb. It's not like choosing clothing fads that can be discarded as easily as chewing gum when that fad has run its course. Medical Alert: Tattooing is permanent skin graffiti!

I know, you think I have it in for those who prefer to brand their bodies with blue ink, right? Well, again, you are exactly right. I think of tattooing very much like I think of smoking. They are both I.Q. tests. I mean, doesn't it seem silly to inflict unnecessary pain on your body? So, when you do — bzzzz! You failed the test! When you light up you might just as well put a sign on your forehead with the word IDIOT on it. It's unhealthy, it stinks, it's addictive, it odor-stains furniture and carpets — and your fingers — it pollutes air, it causes cancer, it's a fire hazard, it makes your teeth yellow and your breath smell like badger guts, it offends others, it leaves burn marks on motel tables and counter tops, and it is not cheap. Other than those few minor drawbacks, it's a very attractive habit.

In the normal course of life, there will be plenty of painful experiences. You don't need to hunt for them.

Both surgery and tattooing are painful, but there's usually a purpose to surgery. However, another advantage of surgery — of any kind — is that you can't see where you had surgery five or ten years later.

I know, you're saying, "But that's the idea of a tattoo. You want it to show."

Do you now? Forever? How about the WW2 vet named Mike who married Maxine. He has a big heart tattooed on his arm, and in the middle of the heart, much to the dislike of Maxine, is the name "Connie," his high school heartthrob. There are millions of such situations, and many much more embarrassing than these.

I know, it's really none of my business. But I am entitled to my opinion, just as you are. If you want to be an idiot and broadcast it to others with overt smoke signals or body paint, go ahead. I won't talk about you too much. I won't even laugh at you for stuffing good money down a rat hole.

Have you checked out the cost of smokes lately? Even the generic brands nearly require a bank wire transfer to the cig shop. And tattoos? I have yet to see a free offer from a tat parlor. Those indelible scribbles cost a good share of your paycheck. (I was going to say an arm and a leg, but if I said that, where would you put the tattoo?)

In sum, it's a free world where we each get to express our own agency and pursue our own dreams, health habits and body decoration. Go for it, you thoroughly modern dudes and dudettes. Reach for that brass ring!

## 18

## *Things That Really Bug Me*

- **People who say one thing and do another (two-facers).** If you don't want to go to the movie with us, just say so. Don't tell us you're sick, and then show up later at the movie with another group of friends. Come out and say you don't wish to go with us. It's okay. We can handle the truth.

- **Tiny lettering on bathroom bottles in motels** (or anywhere, for that matter). I don't usually shower with my reading glasses on, so I can't discern which bottle is shampoo and which bottle is conditioner, or something worse. Is that asking too much?

- **People who blow their nose at the dinner table.** Have we not advanced any in social etiquette since Genghis Khan or his grandson Kublai Khan? I have witnessed nose blowing in restaurants, loud and persistent. Then some blowers have the unmitigated chutzpah to look into their hanky to view their findings! It's pure social ugliness, exactly the opposite of the social refinement that Amy Vanderbilt taught and preached. If she had witnessed anything so barbaric, I am certain she would have sat up in her casket and said, "I've seen it all now, close the lid and let me rest in peace."

- **Tailgaters.** There seems to be far more of them now that I'm retired and deliberately observe the speed limit, even the 25 MPH zones. Who really honors those slug-paced signs anymore? I mean, besides me. Now I live in a retirement development where the speed limit is 15 MPH. I am used to it, but no one tailgates where I live.

- **Not having the correct tool for the job at arm's reach.** This accounts for why I have 9 pairs of pliers, 8 pairs of scissors, and 14 hammers in various places on my property. I know, it's a bit extravagant, but gosh it's really convenient and so efficient.

- **A wet underside of the lid to my 32-ounce mug.** You see, I don't suck my Pepsi through a plastic tube. I drink it. I figure life through a feeding tube will come soon enough, why rush things? Straws are out. Ice chewing is in — for me. So, have you figured this out yet? I pop the lid at frequent intervals, as my palate demands, and take on fluid and ice. If the lid is wet, soda splashes or drips where I don't want it, usually in my lap. Dry lid, baby; no wet!

- **Loud talkers at the gym.** I go to the gym to exercise, not receive a lecture, or a recap of someone's night on the town. If I wanted a lecture or to hear dialog, I'd take a college course or go see a play. My routine calls for a 20-minute sweat breaker on the recumbent bike. During that time, I enjoy reading. Loudmouths and silent reading do not mix well. Is this a sensitivity issue on my part, or a breach of etiquette on theirs? Either way, excessive noise during my reading time bugs me.

- **People who chew with their mouths open.** Do they think others want to see partially masticated chicken and carrots? Do they wish to catch a fly or two this way? Do they know how noisy their habit is? Do they fear closing their mouth to chew may take their talking tongue out of readiness to blurt out a syllable or two? Were they raised with the same rules of etiquette as the loudmouths? Anyway, it's ugly and impolite. And this is coming from a hayseed from Utah. (I don't think this habit could be found among the acceptable manners, mores, and etiquette of Amy Vanderbilt's era.)

- **Wet socks when I am outside or camping**, and I must put my shoes back on to go somewhere. The only option is to go sockless, but that kind of discomfort drives me crazy as well. You say, "Picky, picky." I say, "Pucky, pucky!"

- **People who say to you, "Hey, if you need anything, just call me."** Or, they say, looking at your difficult plight, "Call me if I can do anything for you." The words ring hollow. They could just roll up their sleeves and help — like right now. If I have to call you to get you to help, I don't think you'd come. You are not being sincere. Look, I am here and my car is there with a flat tire. I already told you I have no jack. You have a car that has no flat. Do you think you could add 1 plus 1 and get 2? "Hey, if you need anything, just call me."

- **People who don't know how to use a blackboard effectively.** A blackboard is supposed to be a helpful tool to support your lesson or presentation. If you use it, use it correctly. That means printing or writing with **large, bold letters** so that everyone in the room can read what you have written without a magnifying glass. If you write teeny-tiny letters, then you may as well use a 3 x 5 card with your information written on it.

- **People who laugh at their own jokes BEFORE anyone else laughs.** You see, if what you say is genuinely funny, people will laugh. That's your cue to join in. However, if what you say is not funny, and you're the only one laughing, you look pretty silly. Catch my drift? Ha, ha, ha, ha, ha!

# 19

## *What Ever Happened to Reality?*

It seems like the longer I live, the more the world seems to be out of kilter, off its natural balance. I feel as if the world is out to trick me, fake me out, give me pig iron instead of real steel. Don't you ever feel this way, too?

I know, I know. It all boils down to money. The big push with all companies is "sell the sizzle." Well, whatever happened to the noble desire to simply enjoy the steak? You can't, after all, eat the sizzle! Furthermore, I don't give a holy hoot if my steak has no sizzle; I just want it to be real beef and taste good, and not give me heartburn afterwards.

For those who are a little slow catching my point about our world turning into a third-rate carnival midway scam, let me give you a few graphic examples.

First, look in any modern vehicle's right-side rear-view mirror and you will find written on the base of that mirror, the following words: OBJECTS IN MIRROR ARE CLOSER THAN THEY APPEAR. This simple warning, if that's what it is, raises several questions. How much closer? Twice as close? Only a little closer than reality? In-your-face closer? So, if objects are really closer than the stupid mirror is allowing me to know, what should I do to compensate? Wear glasses that show things farther away? Don't get upset because the tailgater I see really is two miles back and not on my rear bumper? What if I want to see objects exactly as they are? Use only my left mirror? Divide the distance by three? Take the stupid mirror off and forget about things appearing on my right side? What is the car's manufacturer really telling me? That it can't make a mirror to show objects accurately? That danger will sneak up only on the right side of vehicles? That reading what is written on a mirror is more important than seeing what the mirror is supposed to reflect in order to keep me safe? Objects in mirror are closer than they appear. Indeed. Objects in eye are much smaller than they feel, too, but how does that help me to see any better, or to cope with life?

Next, Royce and Marsha Hatch were friends of ours when we were near-newlyweds in St. Louis, Missouri. Royce was a bargain-hunting dental student, Marsha a crackerjack school teacher. One day Royce convinced me to go to the local hardware store to browse for bargains. While I was looking at power tools, he spotted a 12-roll package of toilet tissue for nearly half the price of his usual brand. The rolls appeared to be normal size. I stress the word ***appeared***.

I guess reality told Royce to buy. He was so excited over his purchase of such a plebian item as tush tissue that I thought he was going to invest in T.P. futures. But, alas, he was duped by the big sizzle. When he unwrapped the package so that he could see the "steak," he discovered the center tubes to be about three times the diameter of normal ones, meaning far less tissue.  In fact, about one-third the normal roll. Royce had been hornswoggled by deceptive packaging!

Third, years later I invested in some mail-order shoes that looked very attractive in the catalog.  The description added more to their appeal.  Huh!  They turned out to be made of papier-mâché with a microscopically thin leather veneer.  One day, I barely stubbed my toe on a pile of leaves entering my house and nearly wiped out the entire top of one shoe.  Don't ever buy Haband Shoes.  Besides being poorly constructed, they were about as comfortable as wearing spatulas strapped to your feet — and actually less attractive!  Once again, Haband had a slick sales brochure and I bought their sizzle.  I just wish they hadn't known my address.  No repeat business from me, that's for certain.

Finally, a few years back, my good buddy Mike Hardin and I attended the local county fair.  We were mainly just browsing the booths, looking for any kind of bargain.  A gentleman was there, hawking shoe comfort in the form of some special insoles filled with water.  His pitch seemed entirely plausible (the sizzle). If waterbeds can provide comfort for the entire body, why couldn't insoles filled with water give the feet the same kind of water comfort?  Both of us bought a pair. They lasted about a week and then one day I arrived home and took off my shoes.  "Wow!" I said aloud, "Why is my sock so wet?"  Bingo!  The light went on.  I pulled out the deflated insole, now as useless as a slab of moldy cheese.  I called Mike and asked him how his water insoles were holding up.  Two flats.  Let's get real: only Jesus is capable of walking on water.  I knew that from the get go, but . . .

# 20

## *Hiking in The Sierras*

Throughout the years I have logged more than a few backpacking miles on the odometer of this aging frame. But each and every trip was memorable in its own unique way — and I never once regretted spending time in God's country with family, friends, and a number of scouting groups.

Having grown up against the backdrop of the stunning Wasatch mountains, exploring the equally impressive Sierra Nevada's was a natural attraction during my years living in Northern California. Usually, I would bring a small notebook to journal each trip — a kind of daily travelogue, if you will. Here are the journals from two hikes — raw and unedited.

### *The Pleasanton Hike of 1983*

**Day 1 -- Friday, 7/29**

We drove from the ranger station near Pinecrest about 5-8 more miles to Crabtree Campground.

Parked the vehicles, locked them, unlocked them, as Dave forgot to close the trunk space in station wagon. We filled our water bottles half full from the stream and started for Bear Lake, a 3.9 mile trek.

We hiked from 12:30 to 3:30, with generous rest stops along the way. We were dragging by the time we got to camp. Jared mixed up some cheese and we ate lemonade and melba toast with cheese — not too bad.

Right now Kevin Mahoney, Doug Peterson and Jared are off fishing. Dave Peterson is sacked out in his tent, and the Larsons are on a scouting hike. I am on a pointed piece of granite — ooh, ouch!

We're planning to do 10.3 miles tomorrow. Good luck. 5:11 p.m.

## Day 2 -- Saturday, 7/30

We left Bear Lake at 8:56, hiking in an easterly direction toward Y-Meadow Dam. We hiked over some pretty rough terrain and a lot of snow until about 12:45 when we finally reached the dam. It was pretty tough in parts. Ken Larson led us across narrow ledges and across streams two or three times. Jared slipped coming up one section of granite and bumped his head on a rock. No blood; just a nice abrasion on the forehead.

The food has been outstanding. Last night we had chicken and rice plus a soup and raspberry cobbler, which we washed down with lemon-lime punch. Today's breakfast called for pancakes with syrup and apple sauce.

After lunch we hiked across a lot of snow until we reached Whitesides Meadow at about 3:30 p.m. We could see that the rest of the hike would be on snow. We could not, therefore, pick up and follow a trail. So, after a short pow-wow next to a river with large cakes of ice floating downstream, we decided to return to a pine grove we had hiked through about forty-five minutes earlier. It was the trail head for Trail #5. Also, we decided the rest of the trek, as originally planned back home, probably would not happen. It took us twenty-five minutes to hike back over the snow that one mile.

We set up our tents and had dinner, built a fire, and went to bed.

## Day 3 -- Sunday, 7/31

This is our layover day — our day of rest — and boy do I need it. I feel like someone has flogged me a few stripes with a dead porcupine, or perhaps the tail of a beaver. We're all up now, waiting for each other to get the bear traps down with our food in them so we can start breakfast.

I'm in dire need of a body washing. We're talking sandblasting. Grungy!! How do wild animals keep clean?

We had three very special meetings today. Priesthood was conducted by Kevin and Bro. Peterson gave a good lesson on all the Book of Mormon characters who had taken long treks — Nephi, Lehi, Enos, Mormon, Moroni, and he told a few special stories with each one. Doug helped out by suggesting another name.

Sunday School lesson was given by Bro. Don Larson regarding Charles Anton of Columbia University who fulfilled Isaiah's prophecy by telling Martin Harris, "I cannot read a sealed book." The thing that impressed me with Professor Anton was his stature as a scholar, not in Egyptology as such, but in linguistics. Apparently, he had published some 40 books in his lifetime and was considered to be a first-rate researcher by his colleagues.

Sacrament meeting was conducted by Dave and Don and I blessed the sacrament. Then we had a fine testimony meeting where the spirit was strong. Jared said he wanted to go on a mission like his father had and that made me feel very good. Jared is a fine boy. Everybody stood and bore his testimony of the truthfulness of the gospel. It was a unique and meaningful morning.

## Day 4 -- Monday, August 1, 1983

Hump day. Started with a breakfast of blueberry pancakes and bacon with hot chocolate. (We eat too often and too much!) Jared disagrees. This morning I suggested that Jared shampoo his hair and he agreed. The water was colder than he liked, and he was not very happy about it.

I think about Lois and the other boys a lot up here and think that it would be fun to do this as a family. I wouldn't bring three meals a day, that's for sure.

Last night I made a slingshot by the campfire and that started a new pastime in camp. Everyone has now tried it, but Ken Larson is the resident pro.

Tomorrow we head for Gianelli, then Crab Tree — about nine miles. Then we're going into some lower trails for a few days and that's it.

This two-day layover has been wonderful.

## Day 5 -- Tuesday, August 2, 1983

Before I chronicle the activities of Tuesday, I must give a brief account of yesterday's big activity. Kevin flipped a twig my way, and I flipped one back. Before many more twigs were flung, I had a stick in hand and Kevin was throwing pinecones for me to hit. This led to snowball baseball with Kevin Malone doing most of the bat work. Then a stray snowball got us all into a freewheeling no-sides snowball war which lasted almost an hour. It was a lot of fun as we moved from rock to tree to ravine, trying to protect all flanks while at the same time effectively attacking all sides.

This Morning. . .

We ate ham and eggs and cocoa for breakfast, broke camp, packed up and left at about 9:05 for Crabtree, about 9 miles away.

The trek was mostly on snow and we all got our feet wet — again. After about two and a half hours of hiking, we found ourselves staring over a very steep cliff into a pretty lake. After a rather interesting map and compass session, we decided that we were off course about a half-mile to the south. The lake looked beautiful and inviting, we decided to stay a night anyway. We reasoned that no doubt there would be more people in Crabtree.

We descended.

## Ward-Tipton Hike of 1994

### Day 1 — Sunday, 7-10-94

Left Sonora at about 6:15 am. First stop was in Twain Harte for a bagel and orange juice. Arrived at Bridgeport at 9:30. Scrounged around for film and such, then headed for Twin Lakes, 10 to 15 minutes away. Checked in at campground; got a parking pass, got our hiking shoes on and made ready for the trek. Picked up the Barney Lake Trail at 10:15. Barney Lake was medium-grade climb of 3.9 miles from Twin Lakes, a good hike for the first day, especially for an ol' dog like me who hadn't hiked in about 7 years. Elevation: Twin Lakes -- 7200 feet; Barney Lake -- 8460, net gain of 1260 feet in elevation.

Beautiful flowers all the way up. Mules Ear, Penstemon, Indian Paint Brush, Wild Onions, Asters, Western Azealia's and more. Arrived at Barney Lake at 12:15. Crossed (via dead fall) Robinson Creek scouting for a suitable camp site. Pitched tents and ate lunch. Kool Aid was great; crackers were dry; gummy scorpions were delicious.

Went for a walk along the south side of Barney. On the way back, Dan and I sighted a nest of a Red-Breasted Sapsucker in an old Poplar snag. Mosquitoes were thicker than flies on a deer carcass, but we waited long enough to see parents return with foraged food. Quickly we photographed the nest and adult and got out of there. Nice find!

We all took a walk to the creek for water. Dan used his purifier pump to obtain drinking water. Jay and David tried their hand as well. Not easy, they discovered. We cleaned about 3 gallons, then we noticed a leak in my plastic bag. Last trip for it. Dang.

Lounged and read in tent. Went on exploration hike nearby.

Ate dinner at 6:15 -- Sweet & Sour Chicken -- not bad at all.  Chased meal with hot, and I mean hot, apple cider.  Jay dropped 2 peanut M&Ms in his cup for added flavor.  Looked good to me, so I tried it.  Not too good.  Wrong combo for me.

After clean up, boys went fishing in lake, and Dan and I hiked to a windy ridge to watch, read and escape mosquitoes. Boys fished until almost 9 pm, then joined us on our granite perch.  Dave caught 6 and Jay 2, released them all for another catch.  Stayed on vista point until stars came out.  We found some common constellations, talked about bats a little and then picked our way back to camp in the dark.

Retired at 9:55 pm. All in all, a pretty fulfilling day with nature. The highlight was the Sapsucker's nest.

## Day 2 — Monday, 7-11-94

Awoke at 5 am.  Checked time with flashlight. Survived until 5:30 inside tent, then had to bail out. Arose, noticed how dry it was. No dew at all. Hiked to nearby rock and continued reading "Tuck Everlasting." Saw a deer on way to rock. At 6:05 Dan came by on his way for a nature climb.  He loves to climb and observe nature, two fine hobbies.

The mosquitoes, almost constant companions, were out in platoons last night, but not so bad this morning. The awesome granite landscape rising on either side of me are almost overpowering in magnitude and stature. Our camp site has a stand of poplars, some junipers and a few Western White Pine in it.

The songs from the birds are a soft symphony of nature. Dan spotted a Rosy Finch this morning. Verified it in his book.

Challenging, but beautiful, hike into Peeler Lake, 4.3 miles from Barney Lake with considerable switchback trail the first few miles. I was the caboose, and not really ashamed to bear that title, either. We gained a little over 1,000 feet, as Peeler rests at 9500 feet. Came into the east end of Peeler; the boys already had their lines in the water by the time I caught up. No fish though. We decided to camp at the small alpine lakes SE of Peeler, so did a short cross-country hike to find them. All the while my pack was killing me. Sure didn't feel any lighter than the day before. When we arrived at the scenic, unnamed ponds, we decided that Peeler Lake would have better amenities, like fresh water, so we left for Peeler, again. This time we hiked to extreme SE end and pitched our tents about 50 yards from the sandy beach. We had a pretty stiff wind, keeping the mosquitoes in check. The boys went fishing, hiking and swimming. Dan and I went skinny dipping -- very briefly, especially for me. Sun felt good once out, wind not so good. David caught an 18" Rainbow Trout in the lake. Nice fish!

Lasagna really hit the spot for dinner. Apple sauce was a wonderful dessert. Both were tasty, but not home cooking!

After supper the boys went fishing again. Dan and I hiked over and read and watched the boys and nature until the stinking mosquitoes drove me off. Before they did, however, we spotted a Finch and a Calliope Hummingbird, which seemed to like my orange vest. I returned to the safety of the tent at 8:35, feeling somewhat trapped. The other three returned around 9:30. The mosquitoes welcomed them home!

## Day 3 — Tuesday, 7-12-94

I arose at 6:05; the others about an hour later. Definitely colder last night. Today was pancake day. We ate 25 cinnamon-apple pancakes among us, Jay eating the most with 7. They were very tasty, especially with the real butter and Mrs. Butterworth's syrup on them. I forgot a spatula, but figured out how to flip them using a knife with a fork. Such ingenuity! It only took us two hours to cook them all. Used a bunch of gas in the process.

Dave and Dan climbed to Crown Point, right above us to the east, 11,460 feet. Jay and I decided we'd do it another time. Jay went fishing, and I began to fashion a whiffle ball bat from a limb.

Peeler Lake is gorgeous and the water from the glacier runoff is cold, sparkling and refreshing.

Finished the "bat" for whiffle ball. Jay almost caught a huge fish. Rolled him over in the water, and he was big. Dan and Dave returned at about 1pm. Loafed a while.

At 3:30 we all decided to hike around the lake to sort of work up an appetite. Aside from a few testy spots -- one which required us to wade around a rock point -- it was pretty casual going. (Of course, for me, every step is pure labor.) We made the circle in 90 minutes, 30 faster than we had earlier estimated. We saw five other hikers along the way.

Upon returning to camp, the big game got underway. The elders were determined to school the youngin's in the fine art of whiffle ball. It was a fun, five-inning game in the meadow, but the old men dominated only in form, if that. Jay played steady and never struck out; Dave smacked two dingers, one off the distant granite wall; Dan was looking for help from the bull pen, and I whiffed on Dave's sucker low balls. The boys eeked out a victory 10-4. Okay, they whipped our butts! Dave was overheard talking trash, even after the game was in the bag. He was mouthing this phrase over and over, "We talked the talk, and we walked the walk." Jay was a bit more subtle with his comment, "You guys suck." Dan's only retort was "Every dog has his day." I just asked, "What's for dinner?" "Honey-lime chicken," came the answer.

Mosquitoes were extra bad. All in tents by 8:30. What in the world are mosquitoes good for, anyway? Fish bait. Beyond that, no one could add anything. Come on, wind, where are you?

## Day 4 — Wednesday, 7-13-94

Going home day. We all slept (well, stayed in our tents) late. Didn't sleep much from about 3 am on. Dan and I got up at about the same time -- 8:20. We read in the tents. It was that or get eaten by the lousy mosquitoes, which appeared to be very hungry.

Basically we broke camp, packed up and ate our bagels or cold cereal, depending on whether you were a Ward or a Tipton. We took a few pictures of each other, checked the camp site for debris, and hit the trail at 9:25. Right away Dave asked for the keys to the truck, anticipating that he and Jay would arrive back at the parking area first. Having no argument with that, Dan handed over the keys.

The hike over the little pass to the main trail was strenuous. I just about busted a gut, but I made it. Dan was patient and stopped when I needed a breather, even though he didn't. Thereafter, it was smooth sailing. We made pretty good time coming down. The conversation was rich and varied. I enjoyed it a lot, especially the talk of the background of Tom Jones and his writing of Tracker. Most interesting!

Spoke with several hikers coming up the trail. Always enjoy talking with other like-minded people.

Arrived at the parking lot at 1:10, 3 hours and 45 minutes after first striking out from Peeler Lake. We covered about nine miles on the return trip. Boys were waiting for us, without a drop of perspiration on their bodies. Said they had been there for nearly one hour. How could that be? We had stopped at Barney Lake for about 10 minutes. Otherwise we were striding right along. Oh, for the exuberance and energy of youth.

Once we got our street shoes on, we headed for Bridgeport for a hamburger and drink. I wasn't so interested in the burger as I was the drink. Boy was I thirsty. I got a 32 oz. Cherry-Coke and then got a refill to boot. Very, very good.

Arrived home at about 4:45 p.m., tired but thankful for a good experience with Mother Nature and three great hiking companions. A great day.

**Summary:** The Wards were wonderful to hike and camp with. The highlight of the trip was getting to know them better. I hope the feeling is mutual. The Hoover Wilderness area is a bit more rugged than the Emigrant, which is more familiar to me. I thoroughly enjoyed the hike and hope to return to Hoover before these memories fade away.

***Visiting the Sierras, 2007***

***Kent & Mike Hardin coaching soccer in Sonora, CA ~1989***

## 21

## *All About Smiles*

It's odd how things end up in your possession. I guess it doesn't really matter where the junk came from. Who cares about that? All it means is another trip to the garbage dump or the recycle center or the Salvation Army Thrift Store.

However, the stuff you acquire that you find useful, even come to cherish, now that's another story. Just be sure that you know which is which. A lot of hearts have been broken over people hastily throwing out "junk" which turned out to be a treasure for the new owner.

My father died in 1988. He and Mom had been married for over fifty-six years, and had lived their entire lives not more than a few miles from their birth sites. Before he died his Aunt Becky (Rebecca Tipton Diamond) passed on and left every earthly possession she owned to him, her younger brother's eldest son. She didn't have much by way of material wealth, but she was kind and generous and honest, and she recognized kindness when it was given back to her. This was the primary reason Dad was named in her will. He was one of the few relatives that treated her with respect instead of scorn, kindness instead of snobbery.

It seemed to me that poverty and humbleness had a way of sullying a reputation in the minds of some family members. I am sorry for that, but that's another issue not suited for discussion here. I believe that those who held that rather penurious viewpoint will one day have to answer for it. And that's all that I'll say on the subject.

Aunt Becky, which is what we called her as well, was a thoroughly decent human being despite her threadbare sweaters and coal-blackened fingernails. I don't regret for a second the time my brothers and I spent mowing her lawn, hauling coal or water, fixing a sagging door or helping her in other ways. I only wish I had done more. Looking back, it seems like such a paltry bit of service we rendered. She was always so grateful, and through little acts of kindness showed her generous heart. The truth is: I'd take any of the Aunt Becky's of the world to ten from a family of royalty any day.

But back to my story. When Dad died, naturally my mother inherited his holdings, which included a few meager pieces of furniture and a few books from Great Aunt Becky's estate, if that's what you could call it. Ten years and one month after my father's death, my sweet mother passed on, leaving everything she and Dad had to us four kids. Going through the possessions of deceased loved ones is not an enviable task. It's something that is done every day of the year by families all over this globe, and yet the fact that it is a common ritual does not make it any easier. It truly was one of the most difficult things I have ever done, second only to watching my parents' health waste away and finally die.

We dealt with Mother's death as best we could. A time was set for us to rendezvous in Utah to do what had to be done. Tasks were given out: hauling old trash, sorting garden implements, pruning trees, cleaning closets and bedrooms, disposing of old jars of fruit, boxing up discarded clothing, and so forth. My emotions prevented me from moving through these jobs with dispatch. I'm usually a fast worker, but not this day.

One by one, I would take objects into my hands, stare at them, and then reminisce about how they had been used in our home. I would think about my loving parents who also had caressed this vase, nutcracker, book, or crescent wrench. Looking at photos my mind traveled back over time recreating scenes from my childhood days. *They taught me, loved me, gave me my values,* I thought. Rings, silverware, watches, neckties, and shoes were looked upon with poignant thoughts of the people who once cared for them and wore them. Throughout the process, I was constantly a thin membrane away from tears.

One day, about the third time my siblings and I had met to sort, organize and distribute the household goods, bookshelves and their contents became the focus of our efforts. Dean, my eldest brother, had no interest in them, and quickly waved his right of ownership. Sister Marjorie, who has the same pack rat instincts that I do, wanted some, and we knew that Gary, a professor at a major university who couldn't make this particular trip, also loved books, and so we dealt him in. The books were divided three ways as fairly as a blind lotto, and we each boxed up our treasures and gave them new homes, setting Gary's aside in a secure place. Mine were trucked all the way to California, Marjorie's to her home in Florida.

I didn't know exactly what was in my boxes because the dividing had been done rather quickly. However, once home, I inventoried the books and among them I found one volume that definitely came from Aunt

Becky's estate. It was titled ***Happy Homes and the Hearts that Make Them*** by Samuel Smiles.

On the gift page above three beautiful angels drawn and engraved by Sir J. Reynolds and J. Sartan, I read the words: "Presented To W. M. Tipton By His Mother," meaning William Morton Tipton, two years older than Aunt Becky, and nine years older than my paternal grandfather, Isaac Norman Tipton, who was born the same year this book was published — 1884. William's mother, my great-grandmother, was Frances Sara Winecoop Tipton, born the 25th of October, 1858 in Cincinnati, Ohio. She and my great-grandfather, John Alexander Tipton, raised four sons and a daughter. Two of them, Isaac Norman and John Chester, share my birth town — Springville, Utah.

That I held in my hands a book that was touched and read by ancestors made it that much more personal and meaningful to me. What really struck me with power, however, was what I found inside. The book is a veritable treasure trove of wisdom, morality, and powerful insights designed to help all of us live more productive and happy lives.

I left the book with a bookmark in my little office where it was always within easy grasp and, over the next few years, I chipped away at its contents. It is not a small book by any standards, having 631 pages of text, and so it was not a quick read. After reading about half of it in this sporadic fashion, I decided to attack it head on, and so in 2002 I made it my nightly reading instead of just "filler" reading. I'm glad I did. I finished the last half in less than three weeks. What a tremendous book! And the wisdom from the many snippets of biographies it presents is both breathtaking and interesting. It truly is one of my treasured volumes, one I'll never sell.

After finishing it, I was left with two separate thoughts. First, now that I knew of its contents, I was even more impressed with my ancestors. To think that they wanted to enrich their household with such a literary treasure was touching. And to further ponder that they very likely endeavored to teach their children from it, and encouraged them to read it, was a worthy notion which made me proud. My great-grandfather could easily have sat and fanned the same pages I fanned two generations later.

The second thought I had was: I desperately hope that someone of means reprints the original in its entirety someday, as that is really the best way to enjoy Dr. Smiles and his wisdom.

Perhaps someday you may be lucky enough to come across an original book by Samuel Smiles. If so, buy it and treasure it. It will be one of the best purchases you will ever make, regardless of price.

**NOTE:** As of May 4, 2012, it appears that publisher Editorium has reprinted this book, now available on Amazon. If it's still in stock at the time you read this, order yourself a copy — pronto! You'll be glad you did.

## 22

## *What are the Odds?*

### *A Chance Reunion, 2003*

It had been great getting together with my siblings in Utah, visiting with son Erik, his wife Dusti and their twins, Carter and Riley. We even enjoyed — in a perverse way — jogging in the 5K run Erik had entered us in. But all that was now behind us by a few days. Lois and I were heading back to our home in Sonora, California, our retreat in the foothills.

It was Sunday, June 29. We had pulled into Susanville via Highway 139 from Alturas on Friday. Lois suggested stopping early for the night to give us time to swim and relax. At first I thought she was kidding. She wasn't. So, we checked out this new motel she had seen. Immediately we took a liking to High Country Inn — so much so that we decided to stay two nights instead of one.

When Sunday morning dawned, Lois telephoned the local LDS ward to inquire about meeting times. "Nine o'clock for sacrament meeting," the unknown brother told her. It was 8:15 at the time. I had barely removed the sleepy bugs from my eyes.

Quickly we readied ourselves and drove across town to a handsome chapel. It was a sparsely attended meeting, but the Bishop apparently didn't think so. He welcomed what he saw as "extra" saints and assumed they were relatives who were attending the funeral of Brother Smith, a longtime member of the ward who just passed away days before. It was a good meeting, and it felt good to attend, even though we were among strangers.

With sacrament service behind us we drove back to the motel. Upon pulling into the parking lot in the back, Lois pointed to a white van and said, "Hey those folks attended church with us. I recognize them. They must have come for that Brother Smith's funeral." I glanced up, but her comment of having fellow saints staying at our motel didn't strike me as unusual.

People began emptying from the van. Lois said, "Good morning, it looks like you go to the same church we do." Again, I thought little of her socialness, and truly assumed they were indeed relatives of Brother Smith.

"Thank you," I heard Lois say. I looked ahead and one of the van people, a handsome man in his mid-thirties was holding the door for Lois. I was walking a few yards behind her, and courteously he continued to hold the door for me. As I passed, he looked into my eyes and said, "Devin Samuelson," then gave me at least a sixteen-tooth smile. His eyes were honest and alert, and they complemented his smile nicely.

"Kent Tipton," I said in response to his introduction.

He extended his hand while repeating, "Kent Tipton," seemingly visibly interested in my name.

"T-I-P-T-O-N?" he asked a second time, disbelief settling in his face.

"Yes," I said, shaking his hand, now curious as to why my name would intrigue him so.

"We have a Tipton traveling in our party right now," came his next sentence.

"Wait a minute," I said to him, a few dim lights in the dark recesses of my brain suddenly getting brighter.

"Samuelson did you say? From Phoenix?"

"Yes," this Devin said.

"Marilyn and Wayne Samuelson are your parents?" I queried.

"That's right. They're both with me now," he said.

"So, how are we related?" he asked.

"Your grandfather Bus Tipton," I explained, "and my father Norman Tipton are brothers!"

"I can't believe this!" he exclaimed.

"Neither can I," I agreed.

"Then you're the one who wrote the book about the Springville bank robbery?" he asked.

"Yes. That's me."

"My daughter just read a passage from your book at Young Women last week," he explained. "She was asked to share a story of family history with her class."

"Small world," I said.

"Yes, it is."

Then Devin and I entered the motel and I embraced my first cousin, Devin's mother, Marilyn on the stairwell. We hadn't seen each other in about twenty-five years.

When I returned to our room and explained the whole coincidence to Lois, she listened patiently, then looked at me with those pretty brown eyes of hers, and said like a judge at his bench, "Kent, that's why you go to church."

"Did I say we shouldn't go?" I asked her.

"No, but just remember, that's why you go."

While in Utah on this very trip, my sister Marjorie and I visited Marilyn's mother, Aunt Elva. From that visit we knew that the Glen Tiptons were having a 4th of July reunion in Rexburg, Idaho, home of Marilyn's sister Judy. What I couldn't figure out, however, was why this group of relatives had chosen to travel so far west to Highway 395 in California. I stewed on that odd circumstance while we chatted with them at the motel. Then the explanation came: Devin owned a few acres in Oregon, and they were stopping off for a few nights of camping before venturing northeast into Idaho for their family reunion.

We ended our chance reunion with a few photos of each other, and a few hugs.

Now, I've had some other happenstance occurrences in my life, but this has to be one of the most low-odds strikes of luck I've ever seen. We actually had a mini-family reunion, and no one was even told the time or the meeting place. We just met. What a deal!

## *LDS Chapel, Groveland, October 2011*

It was a Churchwide broadcast concerning the use of the new handbook, "Administering the Church." Lois and I were in attendance. I was asked to arrange the opening hymn, as we thought each local unit was responsible for the music. Lois was to conduct. She asked me what hymn we should sing. I answered, **"How Firm a Foundation**." She countered, "No, let's sing **"Redeemer of Israel**." Since she was conducting the music, I did not argue. The program started and, to our surprise, the opening hymn was already in progress. We didn't need to choose hymns at all. And what was the opening song, being sung Churchwide? **"Redeemer of Israel**."

But that's not all. After the presentation, which was really worthwhile, the broadcast was closed with the hymn, **"How Firm a Foundation**," the very hymns Lois and I had picked.

You just don't forget things like this. What are the odds, pray tell?

## *Jackson Rancheria RV Park, March 2017*

Lois and I were playing Gin Rummy. The first hand I was dealt three kings and seven other cards. The deck was shuffled several times and cut. The second hand I received three kings again. How odd, I thought. Better give this deck a thorough shuffling. And I did. The third hand I was dealt ... is it possible? Yes, three kings again. I immediately showed Lois. We couldn't believe it. Since she knew what I was holding, she won that round.

Really, what are the odds?

## *Chicken Little and Blanche P. Tipton*

"One day Chicken Little was picking up corn in the corn-yard when — whack! a pea fell out of a pea-pod and hit her upon the head." You've heard the story, I'm sure. "The sky's a-going to fall: I must go and tell the King," Chicken Little says. And, you know the rest. This was a story my mother read to my siblings and me as children. In fact, since I am the youngest in my family, I'm guessing that this is the reason she used to call me Chicken Little. It never offended me because I knew my mother was using the term affectionately, and Mother, above all else, dearly, deeply loved her children. So much for backdrop.

Gary and Janet from Mesa, sister Marjorie from Marianna, Florida, Dean and Marie from Springville, Utah and Lois and I from Sonora, California were enjoying our annual reunion in Provo, Utah. The year was 2007; the month, a hot July. We had already had a few laughs, and seen a few sights. We had even visited our two remaining aunts on the Prior side of the family: Aunt LaRue (age 85) and Aunt Susie (age 87), both living together in Aunt Susie's house in Spanish Fork, Utah. It was the second or third day of our get together.

Marjorie and I decided to make a run to the local D.I. (Deseret Industries Thrift Store) to check out books. We both are smitten with this hobby, and apologize to no one for it. In the front of the store is a collectibles center, home for all the "treasures" which had been carefully combed out and adorned with a steeper price tag.

"Hey, let's check out the collectibles?" came Marjorie's voice.

"Yeah, why not?" I replied, and meandered toward her.

A few books caught my eye. They were under lock and key. I petitioned the clerk to open the cupboard. She did. I picked up one, and then another. Then I saw a child's book with the title **Chicken Little** written on the cover. Recognizing the little story at once, I wanted to buy it. I picked it up and opened the front cover. That's when I received the shock of my life!

There in cursive writing was the name Tipton. I was sure this book had come from my family's library. Of course, I bought the well-worn book. It cost me a cool ten bucks.

Later that day I showed the book to both my brothers as well. After thoroughly checking it out, we all agreed that our mother, Blanche P. Tipton, had written the name Tipton. It was her handwriting.

Now, I ask you. What are the odds that a man from California named Tipton could walk into a thrift store 800 miles from home and find a book in which his mother had penned her surname? What is the chance of that happening? The book had been absent from the Tipton home for at least fifty years, and here it shows up in a Tipton's hands again?

What are the odds? Slim, very slim. But, I've always liked long odds.

## 23

## Luck Comes in Threes - I Know That Now

June 16, 2004 was an interesting day for me. It was my first official day of vacation, but I still had to attend a board meeting that evening to present my summary of the year. But all this has nothing to do with what made it interesting.

When my secretary called me to come and write two letters of recommendation I had promised to write, I thought my luck was going against me. I was put out that I still had odds and ends like this hanging over my head. I was ready for some R & R, but these unfinished tasks kept throwing me off track, delaying my annual rest cycle.

Once reunited with my spouse, Lois and I began to do our chores. One of those was to buy a new taillight bulb for my truck. Just outside Kragen's Auto Parts Store I bent down to recover a quarter.

"Lookie here," I said. "It's a bad day when a feller can't find a penny or two."

That was number one.

A few minutes later we were returning to my truck in the Taco Bell parking lot, and sure enough, there on the ground was a nickel. I stooped to claim it.

"Today's my day," I said to Lois, showing her my new treasure.

"That's two in one day."

"You're having a good run," she said. "Maybe you'll strike gold next."

While showering, before getting ready for the board meeting, I decided I would go casual. *It was too hot for long pants*, I thought. *I'll just wear shorts. If anyone objects, I'll just say that I'm on vacation.*

I dried off and trundled off to the extra closet to find a pair of shorts I hadn't already packed for the upcoming cruise. "Hey, there's a pair I haven't worn in a long time." I pulled them out, found a shirt to go with them and slipped into them. I stuck my hands into the pockets to straighten them out. Lo and behold, what did I find in the left front pocket? My lost money clip and the $29 in bills which had been missing since July 26, 2003.

How did I know the precise date? With the money clip were two movie ticket stubs for **Seabiscuit**, the last movie Lois and I had seen. The date was stamped on them. What a deal.

*Number three*, I thought.

Of course, I told Lois. She smiled.

I can't tell my secretary this story because Lois told her about my lost money clip just before Christmas, and she thoughtfully bought me a new one. In one fell swoop that would reverse the whole beneficial effect of her kind act.

Lois was quite unimpressed with all this luck of mine. She said it boiled down to this: having two money clips only doubled my odds of losing one again. I'm trying not to think of her pessimism. I had three lucky strikes in one day, and I was a happy man. However, I'm still looking for that gold. I always am.

## 24

## *Church in Groveland, CA*

Memorial Day weekend, 2003. It was a great idea to escape to the foothills and set our regular activities aside for a few days. Lois and I have always been in unison on the importance of finding time to loaf. We're both hard workers, but coasting is a very important activity, and we know how to loaf really well. Everyone needs a break from this fast-paced life, a change of pace, an easing back on the throttle. It's good for the soul. On this topic we have never argued.

Lois and I made our way up to the cabin on Saturday afternoon after running errands, working out at the gym and doing the necessary weekend packing. We spent a peaceful night watching an off-beat movie, *The Best Man of Shady Creek*, which struck us both as fresh and funny.

Sunday morning, we stopped off at the lake and left the canopy, a few towels and a couple of lawn chairs so the boys could set up "camp" on the beach when they arrived later. Then off to church we went. We sat down and the first thing we noticed was that when the Branch President said, "Good morning" to the congregation, the congregation responded with multiple "Good mornings" right back. That seemed to set the casual mood of worship in this part of God's vineyard.

We noticed several women in pant suits, something we rarely see in our home ward. I looked about the chapel and noticed several men in very casual shirts, one was attired in what looked like khaki desert clothes. But the greatest shock was yet to come.

The sacrament hymn played and we all joined in singing. Soon I looked up and there next to me was a large man with short gray bristles for hair and a receding hairline, receding clear to the crown of his head. He sported a blue, short-sleeved, open necked shirt with a bolo tie. Above the bolo tie was a gray handlebar mustache, extending well below his chin on either side. He extended his hand with the tray in it. I partook and handed the bread to Lois next to me. My eyes couldn't resist completing their tour of his body. His black pants were held snug over his ample belly by two, dark brown, two-inch wide heavy-duty suspenders. What set them off as unusual, however, was not their color or size, but the words printed on them. I did a double take. On his right one, my left, in large block letters was the word HARLEY, vertically written. On his left one, you guessed it, DAVIDSON.

I contemplated what this good brother's life was all about, as I had never been served the sacrament by anyone wearing Harley suspenders. Perhaps he didn't even own a bike. Maybe he just liked suspenders and those two words.

With the sacrament completed, the Branch President stood at the microphone once again and introduced the speakers. The first one spoke. She was the chorister that day, and she gave a wonderful talk on the power of example in our lives.

"And now Brother Travaris will address us," said the good Branch President. From the audience arose a large figure, who ambled to the front. It was the Harley man! Juxtaposed to his casual attire and my impression of him as a wayward motorcycle dude, he quickly whipped out a Macintosh PowerBook computer and proceeded to speak from notes on his screen. He, too, gave a wonderful talk on the evidence of God in nature. He was quite well versed in science, and seemed to love the church a great deal.

This experience taught me the breadth of acceptance and tolerance the Gospel encourages. We are not judged by our outward appearances, but by what is in our hearts. We would all do well to review the importance of this lesson every day we live.

Yes, we'll go back to Groveland. We love that humble little flock of saints.

**P.S.** I just learned today, May 26, 2007, that Bro. Travaris passed away recently. He had numerous health problems he was battling, all as a result of war injuries in Vietnam. May he rest in peace. I hope he knows that I was merely using him as an object lesson for the benefit of all, and not poking fun of him personally. His presence will be missed by the good folks in the Groveland Branch.

## 25

## *Tree Prison*

Retirement is great, it really is. Some senior citizens I know don't agree with me, I can tell by their actions (and occasionally by their words). I mean, when a person who puts in 44 years at a job, retires, and then goes back to work a few months later, what does that tell you? Or when another person with a fat 401K says, "I'm bored and you'll be bored too six months into retirement." Well, guess what? I've been retired now just short of three years and I'm not bored yet. I am very busy doing all kinds of interesting things. Like, well, like . . .

A little over a year and a half after retiring from education, my wife Lois and I spruced up our home a little. I was in charge of the outside department, Lois headed up the department of interior. For starters, I tore out our aging and rotting redwood deck and replaced it with concrete. Whew! That was a chore. About one-third of the wood was still good, and I stacked it out of the way for a few good potential purposes I had in mind.

To get to one of those purposes, I have to take a few steps back into my childhood. Building, inventing, and repairing things took up a good share of my life between puberty and marriage. My buddies and I were constantly framing, fabricating and fashioning some doohickey, usually at my father's property, and sometimes at his expense, as we did destroy property from time to time — not intentionally, only when experiments went sour. Truthfully, that sounds like we were junior engineers of some stripe. How about this: we slapped together many projects which we thought would be monuments to world genius, but turned out to be crap, pure unpolluted c-r-a-p. But, truth to tell, much experience and knowledge were gained in the doing. We soon advanced to where we built better crap, and then even better.

We built a number of huts, tree houses, forts, clubhouses, shelters for the bored, call them what you like. Some were elevated, some were subterranean, and some were combinations, you know, shacks with partial cellars. Some of our work would be praised today in certain quarters — like simple folks of third-world countries, real simple folks, or maybe that throng of homeless folks under that bridge south of town. However, I was never satisfied with any of our slipshod, slap-crap hovels because, for various reasons, we never finished them — NEVER! I've never confessed this, but I have been living with an "Incompletion Complex" for most of my adult life. Deep inside I vowed to build that hut I never built in my youth. It took about five decades for that dormant vow to be awakened, and for that complex to be shattered. Finally, in October of 2007, as I looked upon all that good lumber, redwood lumber, lying in stacks before me, the vow came to life. "I will build a tree house," I said to the lumber. Hearing no objections, I took my declaration to be final.

And that's exactly what I did, about 160 feet from my house, down in the east forty. It has three windows, one of them double pane, a solid door, and a twenty-year roof. But the best part is that it is eight feet off the ground, right next to a 200-year old oak tree. We call it a fort, but I'd bet all the secrets I know about my childhood buddies (and they are considerable) that millions of people in underdeveloped countries would call this fabrication a luxurious pad. Okay, so you have to climb a ladder to enter. So what? Every window has a screen to keep mosquitos and flies out and allow a fresh breeze in. It's 100% redwood. Even the sheathing — solid two-inch sheathing under a long-life roof. Let the foul weather come, baby. Let the rain, sleet and snow fall. I've got my fort to keep me warm.

My son Jay and I built a deck adjoining the tree house. We built it around that old oak tree. It added about 50 square feet of living space to our elevated hut. Of course, being high in the air we had to build a secure railing.

Now, about that door. It needed a doorknob or a latch, or some sort of mechanism to close it and perhaps lock it. So, I installed a nifty little slide-bolt gate lock on it. Metal plate with hole in it on the left jamb; bolt on the right. Now, I am always one to cut things close, so I made sure no space was wasted between bolt and plate. A small flick of the bolt to the left, and whoosh, the door was secure, from the outside, of course. I planned to install a latch of some type on the inside later. The bolt is designed to accept a padlock so that one could lock the bolt shut or lock it open to prevent some prankster from locking someone inside. I could see how a nice combination lock would complete this project.

I was paying so much attention to the locking system that I overlooked a small problem at the bottom of the door. The door rubbed against the threshold and prevented the door from closing cleanly. So out comes the rasp, and down on my knees I go to solve this problem. Of course, I am standing **inside**. How could I fix this standing on air on the outside? The deck was not yet built. I removed what I thought was a sufficient amount of wood from the threshold and then decided to try the door. I vigorously closed it, pushed on the bottom of the door, specifically on that troublesome corner, and tapped the door from bottom to top to see that it was fitting properly. It was. And the door remained shut.

"Well, that's that," I said and swaggered across the small hut to gather my tools.

When I pulled on the handle-less door to get to the ladder and retire for the day, I was mildly shocked. The door was locked, and I mean **locked**.

"This isn't really happening," I said out loud to myself. I felt stupid giving voice to my thoughts, but I was quite isolated.

Fact is, I was 160 feet from the house, so yelling for Lois was out. It was out anyway, because on second thought, Lois was in the next county enjoying dinner with her friend Mary. Further, it was about five o'clock and she didn't plan to be back until around eight. *Wow, three hours in the tree house all by my lonesome,* I thought.

I tried to jimmy the bolt with my screwdriver, but the door was too tight against the door frame. I pried and jiggered, jiggered and pried, but no luck. Who masterminded that tight fit? Of course, Yours Truly. I thought and thought about an escape route. Gosh, I didn't want to break any windows. And eight feet off the ground? I could see myself doing a forward roll and landing on the ground with several broken bones.

*Oh, well, I'll just settle in on a hard seat and read a book,* I thought. *I've got plenty of reading material down here. No big deal.*

Then it hit me. No reading glasses! I had no reading glasses. I detest wasting time — absolutely hate it! I grabbed *Where the Red Fern Grows* off the shelf anyway. Without my glasses I could manage the title, but that was it. I couldn't read the first word.

*Aha! Eureka, baby!* I noticed I had my cell phone with me. *Yes!*

I called my buddy Mike Hardin, who lives just down the street, just a whoop and a holler from me. I dialed his number and prayed he'd answer. He did.

"Mike, boy am I glad you're at home."

"Why's that?" he asked.

"Well, because I have a particular problem that I hope you can help me solve."

"And what is your problem, K.T.?" he asked.

He called me K.T.W.T. quite often. I called him Hardini or Bubba Louie. They were just affectionate nicknames, that's all. I have never known the meaning of the W.T. One day I'll ask him, I suppose.

Well, I explained in detail my predicament. He laughed — a full belly laugh.

"So, let me see if I've got this right," he said between chuckles. "You're eight feet in the air, locked in a tree house of your own design, and you can't get out. Have I got it right?"

"That's about it," I told him.

"Lois must be happy about that arrangement," he said.

"Lois is miles and miles away, so I don't know what her reaction may have been, but you're probably right. She would likely appreciate my confinement," I explained. "So, can you come down and let me out of my prison, or do I call 911?"

"Sure, I think I can."

"What do you mean you ***think*** you can?" I asked.

"Well, we just came in off the lake, and I've got to unload our gear, and then I've got to clean the boat, then Joan wants me to run to the store and pick up a couple of steaks for our dinner, and then . . ."

"So, when can you come?" I cut in, rather rudely I am sorry to confess.

"Oh, I'd say . . . Let's see, if I hurry, I can probably make it in two, two and a half hours, maybe three."

By then I suspected he was pulling my leg. Then he chuckled and I knew for sure he was putting me on. "I'll be right down," he said.

When he arrived, we had another hearty cackle as I showed him how the bolt had jiggled into the locking position as I tapped on the door to see if all was right. Mike was my hero that day, no doubt about it. He set me free!

When Lois arrived home later that night, I told her the whole story and she too chortled. Then she said, "I knew I shouldn't have left you at home alone. You have a natural knack for getting into trouble, you big dummy."

Her words really soothed me.

Next morning I was tempted to lace her hot chocolate with pepper, but then I thought, *hey, at least I'm free*, and I brewed her a really rich cup of cocoa.

*Kent & siblings Marjorie, Gary & Dean, 2017*

*Kent & Lois on Maui at sunset, 2017*

# 26

## *The Courage to Carry On*

Let me tell you about Mrs. Hencely — or Sister Hencely. A happy-go-lucky Utah-born woman, she married a Southerner, who also liked to laugh. They had two fine, hefty sons. She and her hubby raised these two boys in the Church and, when they came of age, they elected to serve missions, which pleased their parents.

Life was good. Sister Hencely maintained a bounce in her step and a smile on her face. For years, even decades, things went along swimmingly until her husband's diabetes progressed rapidly. Doctor's visits; treatment in the hospital; and sick leave became routine. Then surgery on his feet, taking the toes first, then amputation of one foot, then up the leg, one piece at a time. It was only a matter of time now. That time came July 2, 1997. Charles had planned his own funeral, and it came off well, just as he wanted it. There were tears aplenty. Sister Hencely clung to the Church and her two sons for support. She prayed for help, and received it. She learned to live without a husband. It wasn't easy. She put one foot in front of the other, never complained, and carried on.

A year and a half later, 1998, on Christmas Eve, of all times, her dear mother passed away. Since Sister

Hencely was the only daughter of five children, she had enjoyed a special relationship with her mother that her four brothers just didn't have. They giggled and laughed together as only girls can do. She traveled to Utah, attended the funeral, cried some more, and then she returned to her home in Florida with her two sons. For weeks, she cried many nights calling up memories of times with her mother. And she prayed mightily. Then, she cried and cried some more until she was out of tears. Then she carried on.

September 11, 2000 rolled around. It was a beautiful day. Sister Hencely had a smile on her face as she drove to work. Her oldest son Wes needed to travel to Tallahassee to renew a teaching credential. But he never completed that journey. Wes was killed in a freak accident on the freeway. Killed on impact. He left an infant daughter, a disbelieving wife, and a grief-stricken mother. Widow and mother cried some more. Through their tears they prayed for understanding. This loss was really tough for mother because Wes had been her firstborn and had always been full of cheer and sunshine, which he freely shared with others. But, after heartache and tears, Sister Hencely straightened her spine, threw her head back, reclaimed her smile, and carried on.

Two weeks later she received word that Wes's cousin Tracy passed away unexpectedly. He was five years younger than Wes. This death sent a shock wave through her whole family. Sister Hencely sent her sympathies to her brother, the father of Tracy, cried and prayed some more, and then — she carried on.

But the full weight of tragedy had not yet fallen upon Sister Hencely. There was more to come.

December 23, 2000 (same year), her remaining son went in for surgery. The procedure was a success. But in the recovery room John developed a blood clot and it took his life — just like that. I cannot describe the depth of the valley of sorrow that Sister Hencely fell in to, but it was deep. Even though she never complained, the weight of this fifth family loss was too much for her.

From the date of the death of her husband Charles, to the death of her last child, John, a mere 42 months on the calendar had expired, three and one-half years. The burden of sorrow was accumulating, stacking up, death by death.

After John's funeral, Sister Hencely could not imagine how life could get any rougher for her. But that thought did not erase her emotional burden. She needed additional help. Her understanding doctor prescribed a safe medication for depression. She took it, immersed herself in her church work — and carried on. In time she returned to life without medication.

I know this story really well because Sister Hencely is my beloved sister Marjorie. To me she demonstrates — in real, day-to-day terms — what it means to muster courage to carry on. And she has done it without pity parties and with an infectious smile on her countenance.

Would that I could be that strong.

# 27

# *Red Tape*

Back in November of 2011, I went to the doctor. The receptionist gave me one of those huge forms to fill out wherein they expect you to spill your guts about everything from medications you are currently taking to pregnancy and lactation issues. I don't know why, but I was in a particularly snappish mood. Maybe I was feeling rebellious about having too many doctor appointments lately. Perhaps it was the date — 11-11-11. And it was a Friday. It seems that many spooky, goofy, and odd things happen on Fridays. I didn't know I had any particular hatred for the number 11, but something was off in my mental state, something awry in my bio-rhythm. Perhaps it was the fact that this was Veteran's Day, and I expect to be free on that day, being a vet and all.

At any rate, I continued to answer the questions on the hefty form. After answering a bold "NO" to the question, "Have you ever taken tranquilizers, sleeping pills, anti-depressants, and/or narcotics on a regular basis?" I was insulted because I am no druggy, and I began to get a little steamed. Then after 13 more questions about allergies, the questionnaire then asked, "Please list any allergies other than drug allergies." So, I gave them a list. I wrote, and I quote exactly: "Lazy people, ungrateful people, cheaters, squealers, stealers, and liars."

Just before the emergency contact information, there was this question: "Do you wish to speak to the doctor privately about anything?" I replied, "Yes, that's why I am here." I signed it, dated it, and turned it in to the woman who gave it to me.

I know, you're wondering how the doctor responded to my smart aleck responses, right? Well, either he never read it, which wouldn't surprise me, or he just shrugged it off, and took me to be a real wisenheimer. Truthfully, I felt good about my responses. I answered exactly in concert with how I felt at the time, and that is that.

So much for red tape.

# 28

## *Nailed!*

It was Friday, May 24, 2014. Daylight had given way to night. It was time for bed. I sat on the bathroom counter brushing my teeth, casting my eyes about at everything and nothing. Then something caught my eye. I spat out the toothpaste and called out, "Hey, Lois, what's this stain on the bathroom floor?"

"I have no idea," my wife replied as she came in to examine. "It was clean this morning when I was in here." Being a very conscientious housewife, she immediately grabbed a rag and moved in on the smear. Kneeling down she said, "It looks like blood."

"Who the heck is bleeding?" I asked in all innocence. Then I looked down at my feet, still clad in socks. My right sock had a huge red stain on it. "Whoa! What's this?" I said. Lois glanced at my right foot and was equally shocked.

Let's leave the story there and back up the clock about twelve hours.

The sun was bright; the sky was blue. The morning showed strong promise of plenty of heat later in the day. A jackrabbit bounded across my line of vision, roaming free in the Ridgewood subdivision. I was meeting with a surveyor and a real estate agent. Objective: to flag the corners of our 5-acre parcel so that the agent could show prospective buyers the outline of the lot.

Mike Hardin and I had owned the parcel since the 1980s, and we had just listed it — once again. Years ago, after building a nice access road, we had set up a barrier at the base of the property, constructed of a cable, scrap two by fours, and part of an old picnic table built by my neighbor, Hank Tamerlane. While not beautiful, it functioned well as a crude barricade, sufficiently heavy to keep out most would-be trespassers. We soon learned that it also inconvenienced the owners every time we visited the property. A good Master Lock was the final element needed to secure the property. By the way, this barrier also served as the gateway to our two 20-acre parcels at the end of the asphalt driveway.

When our agent first saw the property, the first thing she said was not about the land at all. She said matter-of-factly, "Can we get rid of your 'security barrier?' " I tried not to take offense, as it represented some of my handiwork, not my best work, but my work just the same. I agreed that I would consider getting rid of it. It was time to go to work. The agent introduced me to the surveyor. He was the picture of action.

He pulled out all his paraphernalia, adjusted his belt with machete hanging from it, threw his transit over his shoulder, and the march through the poison oak-laden jungle began. A mere hundred yards down the trail convinced me that I would not be able to keep up with our much younger surveyor in walking the five acres. I returned to the front of the property to ponder the agent's comments about the barrier. Looking at its ugly form, it took me only three seconds to agree with her. It had to go. So, I retrieved a hammer and screwdriver from my truck and began to dismantle it, board by board, nail by nail. In the process of ripping and prying, I accidentally stepped on a nail. The nail tore away from the board and stayed in the outside of my right foot, halfway between toes and heel.

Did I mention I have peripheral neuropathy? Well, I do.

The fact is: my feet have the sensitivity of a pair of shoetrees. Every now and then my doctor reminds me of this. He usually strikes a tuning fork to set it to vibrating and then he places it on my toenails, one by one and asks if I can feel it. The big toes are as dead as the toes of a wooden Indian in front of a cigar shop. The baby toes have some sensation. The nerves in the bottom of both feet are pretty well shot, shall we say, and the deadness reaches up to the sides of my feet.

By now you are surely ahead of me in my story. That's right. I couldn't feel the nail as it entered my foot. Shortly after picking up a little extra iron, rusty iron at that, I finished throwing all the wood in my truck and decided to hike up the hill a few hundred yards to see if I could see any sign of the surveyor or the agent. Remember, the nail was sticking about a half-inch into my foot as I hiked up the hill. I remember vaguely thinking about why the orthotic in my right shoe was becoming a little uncomfortable, but I never stopped to check it.

The first sign I saw was that of a large, muddy cat track right in the middle of the asphalt road. "That's some tomcat," I jested to myself, knowing full well that it was a track of a sizeable cougar. The next sign I saw was Jan, the agent, fighting her way through the dense underbrush. She finally climbed her way to where I was standing. I pointed out the cat track. We talked for a few minutes, and then I decided to head on home. Down the hill I walked, oblivious to the nail in my shoe and foot. When I arrived home, I puttered in the garage for an hour or more, and then decided to go inside and take a shower. I threw my dirty clothes in the hamper. After the shower I dressed and put on a clean pair of socks, then I put on the same shoes again. As I slipped on my right shoe, the nail reentered my foot in about the same location as the first hole. I wore those shoes — with the rusty nail — for the remainder of the morning. At about 12:30 I walked out to the office for my daily nap. I again took off my shoes and napped for a few minutes. I then put on my shoes. The nail, for the third time, pierced the flesh of my right foot. I did sundry tasks around the yard, walking here and there as needed. Later, we drove downtown to get a yogurt, walking about a block to accomplish that. The spike was still poking me. Then we returned home and watched a movie; I kept my shoes on. Finally, about 9 or 9:30 I took my shoes off and prepared for bed. It was time to brush my teeth.

Now we have come full circle.

Ripping off the red sock, I asked my wife to look at my foot.

"You've got a hole in the side of your foot, that's for sure," she observed.

I got to thinking about how that may have happened. Then I went to the clothes hamper and pulled out my socks I had worn in the morning. Sure enough, there was a telltale red stain on the right sock. Next, I went to my right shoe. Bingo! The offending nail was still stuck in the shoe. I pulled it out and shook my head.

How in the world could I not have felt this spike in my foot all day long? I asked myself. The nail was nasty looking, old and broken in half from decay, but about an inch and a half remained, and the end was very sharp, and very rusty.

It was probably a nail that Hank had pounded himself some thirty years ago when he built that picnic table in the first place. Well, I sure couldn't blame him for my situation.

You've heard of a dumb-dumb, right? Well, I guess you can just call me a numb-numb!

# 29

## *Excerpts from the Heart*

I am a big believer in keeping a journal and visiting it often to record one's most personal thoughts, insights, triumphs, and challenges. The key word here, however, is 'often.' And therein lies the rub. Because, not unlike most of us, I too am guilty of being somewhat hit and miss in the pursuit of this endeavor throughout the course of my life. However, my shortcomings in consistent journal entries notwithstanding, I recently cracked open a few of my personal volumes and was struck by a number of the entries I found. I share them now with you, dear reader, as a brief window into my most honest and heartfelt feelings about country, family, and the wonderful gift of life.

### *January 7, 1974*

Jared is now 4 years and 2 months and about 15 days old. And, he is a very sensitive boy. That is, he laughs at silly, little things; and he cries also over little affairs. He is very precise in his speech patterns. Uses past tenses of verbs with surprising accuracy and has a rich vocabulary. Of course, as 1/2 of the parents, I'd like to think I had a little to do with all his learning. Socially, Jared is very well accepted by his peers. He plays well with others and has an advanced understanding of the concept "sharing." I'm sure Jared will not be a physical giant, but what he may not have in height or weight, he'll make up in charm, good-looks, and lots of smarts. I also peg Jared as a future shortstop on the high school team. He is well coordinated.

Erik — He is now 2 days short of 22 months, and wow! He is Big, Good-Natured, but Stubborn!! His feelings are deep. He is a defiant little pup. But, oh how we love him. And his cute little antics melt your heart away. Tonight, he was trying to tell us he had to go potty and to take his diaper off so he could use the toilet. Result? — dumb Mommy & Daddy just took off the diaper and sat there. Erik peeweed on the kitchen floor.

## *June 27, 1982*

Erik said a funny thing tonight at dinner. He asked me, "Dad, what do you do at work?" (This followed a brief discussion about Grandpa T's construction work.) "Well," I responded, "I spend most of my time in meetings and making decisions, I guess." He came back with, "What kind of decisions, like whether or not the U.S. should bomb Russia?" We all enjoyed a good laugh over that. He is very spontaneous most of the time. All in all it's a joy having 4 boys.

## *July 25, 1982*

I had a chance today (took the time today) to talk with each of the boys — Jared, Shane, Erik and Jay, in that order. Here are some of the challenges I issued each one.

**Jared** - 1.) Plan a way to diminish the arguing with Erik. Don't be a reactor to Erik's alarming statements, but give Erik attention and love when he seeks it. 2.) Throw out all words inappropriate for Jay's little ears — i.e., be an example to his younger brothers. 3.) Treat his Mom better.

**Shane** - 1.) Control temper, not yell at Jay and Mom so much. 2.) Don't tease little Jay.

**Erik** - 1.) Getting along better with Jared. Don't worry about those things which Jared receives solely because of his age position in the family, and always remember we love him just as much as Jared or the other boys. 2.) Treating his mother better. I challenged him to give her lots of love this week. Erik has great potential and a special unique niche in our family.

**Jay** - 1.) Yelling at his mommy and 2.) doing his duties without being reminded. Jay really is a lot of fun. He loves bedtime stories — anytime. Last night I read him 4 and he conned me into one more as I lay next to him after the lights were out. He loves stories of animals, those with a little humor, and especially stories about candy or sweets. Being a basic sweet food junkie, Jay really enjoys sweet stories. Forget pirate's sword fighting over troves of King's jewelry, or cowboys finding the hidden vein of gold. Jay just wants to hear about the magic chest bursting at the hinges with bubblegum, M&Ms, chocolate chips, marshmallows and certs! He's a joy. He just sits there and salivates as his little mind paints vivid pictures of tantalizingly sweet goodies jumping from their wrapper into his mouth. He'd do anything for a little sugar fix, and that is of more than a minor concern.

## *August 2, 1982*

### *Camping at Richardson's Grove, Redwoods*

The boys are really pretty good campers. They love the outdoors and find plenty of nature's wonders to fill their time productively. Jay enjoys hiking and wandering to other campsites looking for playmates; Shane loves to look for frogs, tadpoles and fish at the river; Jared loves to jump off the rocks at his favorite swimming hole; and Erik most loves trying to catch that "King" fish, the one that's been there waiting for his lure for 20 years, but he also loves to swim. Erik is also a very good scrounge — wood, things people left at the campground, you name it.

## *January 2, 1983*

Jared is 13, Erik is 10, Shane 8 and Jay 4 1/2. Lois just turned 36 in November and I'm creeping toward 41 in September. Our family of boys is a family of activity, brimming with loud voices and raucous gaming. Lois likes order and so do I, so raising 4 boys full of zim, zip, vigor and vitality is quite unlike going to a funeral. And yet, while the parents may complain a little here and there, the joy of having 4 healthy boys is one beyond explanation. The benefits and pluses far outweigh the negatives, so the net of it all is joy. Example is such a potent force, such a strong teacher that you have to constantly be on guard that what you do and say may be copied by your offspring without any worry of adverse consequences.

## *November 13, 1983*

I'm home from church with 2 sick boys — Jay and Shane. They're watching a Shirley Temple movie, while I'm getting caught up on a few odds and ends. I hate to consider writing in this journal as a trivial or miscellaneous activity, but somehow, not by choice, it gets relegated to less than an important matter. Perhaps my life is so full of urgent things, I can never get to the important!

Shane and Jay, who are home with me today, are my two most enthusiastic athletes. Both love soccer. Shane plays on a competition team (Al Caffodio U-10 A team — United) and Jay plays U-6 house league under his father as coach. Jay loves to play. Yesterday all games were cancelled due to rain and Jay was so disappointed he cried. It's just as well the weather was foul because Jay is not well right now. Anyway, back to the story. Jay woke up yesterday understanding he had no soccer game, but he couldn't take going more than 7 days without the friendly feel of his uniform draped on his little 45-pound frame. On went the jersey with JAY on the back just above the number 11. Next the black shorts with the BUSC patch on the left thigh. "Surely," I thought, "he won't go all the way." WRONG! Shinguards, yellow socks and soccer shoes were quickly secured on his legs and he was ready. Well, it did help his psyche some to be able to wear his little Bronco outfit. (I mean, if you can't play, at least look like you're getting ready to, right?)

Jared was just ordained a Teacher by his father, two weeks ago — October 30th. He is a special boy with terrific art talent and a great desire to read--mostly sci-fiction and horror stories, but he's reading, at least.

Erik loves thrills, spills and chills. Loves to venture out to the unknown and shows no hesitation about testing the limits we have imposed upon him. We love him dearly, but only hope his brazenly ways will not cause us any undue grief later on. We hope Erik is able to channel his energies properly. If so, he'll be an awesome missionary. Erik's latest trick was to respond by telephone to a TV ad for a record club. He joined over the phone and had no idea why what he had done was inappropriate. All he could see were 11 FREE Albums or tapes. Somehow, some way, he'll pull it all together.

## April 29, 1984

Last nite I had the opportunity to give the boys a little good nite kiss, after being out of town for a few days. When I went into Shane and Jay's room, I stretched my neck up to the upper bunk bed and in a soft voice I said, "Jay, I have a secret to tell you." He raised up to hear. I continued, "I love you." He said, "Dad, I have a secret to tell you." Oh, good I thought. Give a little love and you'll get it right back. He came closer to my ear, his little lips ready to share his secret and my heart ready to receive his message of affection. He spoke, "When are soccer tryouts?" I smiled as I told him in 4 or 5 weeks.

He's a real soccer boy, believe me.

Speaking of soccer, Shane made the Al Caffodio B team for next year. Woody Netheimer is the coach and we're real proud of him.

## July 12, 1984

Erik said a funny thing the other day. He was looking for some chopsticks to eat with and he said, "Dad, now I know what's wrong with chopsticks." And I said, "Oh, what?" And he continued, "You can't tell which one is the spoon and which one is the fork."

Jared and Erik had a good time at Scout Camp Oljato. They were excited about all the unique things they learned (in addition to 8 merit badges, 4 each). Erik earned these merit badges: canoeing, leather work, pottery and printing.

He silk screened several shirts and towels. His favorite activity was canoeing on the lake. All in all both had fun.

## *January 19, 1986*

At this time my heart is filled with thanks for all of these blessings: My wonderful wife, who untiringly works with me in the business and still keeps a tidy house for us; my good health and the good health of my family; my opportunities to build a business and a land that encourages free enterprise; my boys in all their uniqueness. I love them dearly. Jay right now is by my side writing in his journal, too. Erik is at church for B.Y.C., Shane and Lois are in L.A. at a soccer tourney and Jared is all cleaned up and waiting to go to church. More later. KT

## *November 1, 1987*

Today is Fast Day. Jared has been called to be 1st Assistant to the Bishop in the Priest's Quorum. I'm happy for him, and I hope he will consider the tremendous trust the Bishop has placed in him. I am looking forward to working with him as Quorum Adviser. He'll be a great President.

Erik is having a good experience playing JV football. As #67, he plays weak side Def. end and loves it. Friday against East Union, he recovered an onside kick. Unfortunately, they lost 20-22, but it was a very good game.

Football for Shane has been good, too. Shane had 5 tackles yesterday against Galt as def corner back. He also played a little quarterback.

Jay scored 2 more goals in a 4-0 win yesterday as well. He has made a lot of great passes and goals.

## *March 24, 1991*

Our church basketball team (youth) did okay this year. During league play we beat all the easy teams and scared all the tough ones. Erik, Shane, and even Jay played. Where we really shone was in the post season tourney. We beat Riverbank on Tuesday, and Jay scored 12 points (5-6 from the field) and 1 of 2 from the line. Then we beat Modesto 5th, the Modesto 7th, then we met them again in the championship game and beat them again for the 1st place title. Rich Lemon, Alan Lemon, John Bettencamp, Bryan Beck, Cody Lewis, and Kelly Chamberlain were the other players. Beck and R. Lemon were our bread and butter tandem.

## *September 22, 1992*

A few tough days! Saturday, 9-19-92 we received word from a hospital in Idaho that our son, Shane, had been shot in a gun accident. Jay took the call and the nurse wouldn't give details. When I got home from the hardware store, Jay said, "Shane's been in an accident."
"What kind of accident?"
"I don't know."
"What's the number, I'll call and find out."
"They didn't leave one. The nurse said she'd call right back."
A million thoughts crossed my mind in those next 5 or 10 minutes, all of them bad. Car accident? Climbing accident? What kind of accident? How is he? Is it his arm, leg or head that is injured? etc.

Finally, the nurse called back and gave some details. Shane had been shot accidentally by his friend at close range with a .22 caliber rifle. They were in a remote area near Idaho Falls hunting.

They called Med-Flight and got him to the hospital. His lung had collapsed, and he was losing some blood. The bullet had entered his back just under the scapula, pierced his right lung and exited about 2" above his nipple. The doctor put a tube in the lower chest cavity to drain off unwanted fluids, continued the IV and got him X-rayed.

Today, three days later, he is out of the ICU, and doing miraculously well. I'm leaving tomorrow to visit him. His mother, at Science Camp in Point Reyes with her sixth-grade class, would rather be in Idaho Falls, believe me.

Is he recovering solely because of timely and skilled medical action? No, but that helped. The young men gave Shane a blessing before Med-Flight arrived. The power of the Priesthood was at work in preserving and protecting Shane. What a blessing! We thank God for preserving his life. He is a very special young man, believe me.

In thinking about this challenge on Shane's life, I am forced to think about one of my favorite poems:

*Good timber does not grow in ease,*
*The stronger the wind, the tougher the trees;*
*The farther the sky, the greater the length;*
*The more the storm, the more the strength;*
*By sun and cold, by rain and snow,*
*In tree or man good timber grows.*

*- Anonymous*

And Shane is mighty fine timber!

## *July, 4, 1993*

Independence Day. I have only a few short thoughts for this occasion. I am extremely happy I was born in this great land. I love America and all that she stands for. I still get goosebumps when I hear our National Anthem; I still enjoy saying the Pledge of Allegiance; I still have a soft spot in my heart for all the sacrifices our forefathers made for us and I can get a big lump in my throat when I hear of success stories by people who come to this country and make good. I am also grateful for my parents who have given me so much, but especially their love and support and their good name.

## October 3, 1993

Yesterday we had a bonanza day with letters from our missionaries. Erik wrote, and Shane did also. And Shane's missionary friend, Elder Morrison from Tasmania also wrote. It was wonderful. Particularly great was the special letter Erik wrote to Lois. The gratitude and love he expressed for his sweet mother brought tears to my eyes. He has grown so much! We are just so happy both Erik and Shane are in the mission field, bringing the Gospel to deserving souls. The taste of success has been enjoyed by both and trials have come to each. We, as a family, would not trade the joy of this experience for anything — past or future. It is absolutely terrific to have these young men serving in the Lord's vineyard, where joy can be brought to so many others and love can be shared. It is wonderful beyond the power of words to describe.

## August 15, 1997

Right now we're traveling to Elko, NV to exchange cars with Erik (his '83 Honda Accord for our '96 Nissan Altima), something Erik is very anxious about and has been working on for over 18 months. Today it happens.

A few months ago, Erik was in a terrible accident (auto rollover in Scipio, Utah). He was in the backseat. He lost 2 fingers on his left hand. He has handled it with strength, and has been a real inspiration to us all. Lois and I went to be with him and bring him home from the hospital. Then Lois went back to be with him for a week. Our nerves are frayed. We give thanks to God for preserving Erik's life.

Jay landed a wonderful basketball scholarship at Fresno Pacific University (N.A.I.A. Div. 1). We are all excited over this. He has worked hard to do this! About 85% paid!

Jared graduated from Stanislaus State Turlock in May in Organizational Communications with a minor in Journalism. He's now job hunting. We're all hoping he lands something that he's interested in and that will pay him sufficiently for his talents.

## *February 6, 2000*

Wow!! Keri and Shane had #1 Sunday morning at 2:12 am on February 6.

Weight: 9 pounds 3 1/2 oz!!! Wow! Length 22 inches. Head: 13 1/2; Chest 14 1/4; Dr Matt Personius; Sonora Birth Center. BOY! BOY! BOY!

Name: Connor Wyatt Tipton

Excitement is the emotion of the day! What fun!

## September 3, 2001

Good news! Today at 12:45 pm and 12:48 pm, Dusti, Erik's wife, gave birth to two little boys -- Twinkie #1 and Twinkie #2. One was 4 pounds even; the other 4 pounds 7 ounces. Erik assisted by cutting the umbilical cord on each. Length 17". Hooray!! About 2 1/2 hours of labor! This will be a Labor Day Dusti and Erik will remember with special fondness, especially Dusti.

Names: 4 pounder: Riley Kent Tipton, 4 pounder + 7 oz. is Carter Jay Tipton.   C.J. is on a ventilator, helping him breathe. They plan to take it off tomorrow. This little event effectively doubled our count of grandchildren. Wow! Just like that! JOY! JOY!

## *November 9, 2003*

Jared was so proud of his wife and new son. His nervousness and tension showed through his telephone call to us. It was a happy tension that Lois and I enjoyed. Jared also was relieved, I think. Relieved that his son was whole and healthy. Relieved that he had a son to carry on his family name.

Jared is my first-born. I well remember how proud I was that Lois and I were able to conceive and have such a beautiful son. I think most fathers enjoy having a male through whom the surname can be perpetuated.

I hope we'll always be filled with joy and wonder as each grandchild enters our children's homes. Jay and Jenny are next, but they have schooling to conclude first.

We are so proud of all our sons, daughters-in-law and grandchildren. We count these 14 people as our most precious blessings. What a joy it is to be grandparents for the sixth time. Hooray for baby Jacob!

## *January 13, 2012*

Life is good. I pray it is equally as good for my siblings and children and grandchildren. Life is what you make of it, that's for sure. You must work at being happy, and happiness, after all, is paramount. I wouldn't trade places with many, many people of wealth. I have yet to see evidence -- real, convincing evidence -- that wealth creates or sustains happiness.

If you do your very best at trying to make the world better by making yourself better, you will be satisfied with your lot.

> *"Why build these cities glorious*
> *When man unbuilded goes?*
> *In vain we build the world*
> *Unless the builder also grows."*

That little rhyme popped into my head, and it is appropriate. We must work each day to build ourselves, and in turn we will build the world. The year 2012 is going to be an awesome year. I can feel it in my bones. Thank God I am alive to see my ten precious grandchildren reach out and grasp life with both hands. What a lucky man I am to be alive today. Each day is a miracle. What marvelous wonder will tomorrow deliver to me?

## *August 5, 2012*

Yesterday, Lois and I met Jared in Walnut Creek to attend Matt Lyon's funeral. It was a wonderful occasion, absolutely wonderful. Tyler Norton, a former missionary companion delivered the most stunning, inspiring and even poetic, eulogy I've ever heard. It was truly outstanding! We saw Nick, Christian and Dan. I came away with a greater appreciation for my own life and for my sons, their spouses and our precious grandchildren. Often funerals make you sad and reflective, but somehow this one had a particularly more powerful dimension to it. Perhaps, I'm thinking, that its poignancy arose from the fact that I too had a 42 year old son who was once Matt's best friend. Yes, I think this fact had a large part in shaping my feelings yesterday.

Thank God for family; I am particularly grateful for a dutiful son in Jared. May he live a long and joyous life.

## *August 13, 2012*

Well, it happened! Jenny and Jay have a new son, Noah Jay Tipton, 8 lbs - 6 oz, 21" long. Born in Bountiful, Utah. And guess where we're going as soon as we return home from San Gabriel? That's right — Bountiful. Mom and babe are doing well. Hannah and Isaac are excited. And so are we. Wow, 11 little grandchildren. Amazing!

## *November 11, 2012*

Life goes on. Aging is as natural as sunrises and weeds growing. The body wears out, here a part, there a part. Whoever said, "You're only as old as you think you are" was definitely a young whipper-snapper, or someone totally off his rocker.

Being married to Lois is an awesome experience. She is an amazing wife, an effective mother, and a very loving grandmother. I love her for many, many reasons, but one of the key reasons is her simple straightforward groundedness. She does not put on airs. She is comfortable in her own skin, and I never have to guess the difference between her words and her heart, because they are the same. What an incredible woman!

## *November 11, 2015*

### A Little Prayer on Veteran's Day

*- by Kent Tipton*

Thank you, dear Lord, for allowing me to serve my country safely. And thank you for watching over me the entire time I served. While I was not deployed to a combat area, I would have willingly gone. I learned much in the army.

Thank you for patriotic parents who lived through the hard times of both the Great Depression and World War Two, and who understood the necessity of war to keep our generous country safe.

Thank you for a grateful heart that is filled with growing love for a country that is founded on divine principles of law and order, freedom and liberty, respect and dignity, and opportunity and fair play for one and all.

I am proud to be born an American, and I understand that this birthright is not a free pass to snobbery and arrogance, but an obligation to reach out and help those less fortunate to find their dream, and fulfill their divine destiny as children of thine just like I am a child of God as well. Amen

## *December 15, 2017*

Vidalia, Louisiana, ya'll, just across the river from Natchez, Mississippi. We are at a lovely RV Park, River View RV Park & Resort. We pulled in here 6 days ago, planning to stay 2 nights, and we liked it so much we added six more days to our residence on the river.

Amenities: excellent full view of the MS River with all its commerce, hot tub (Wooee!), clean showers, if we choose to use them instead of our own, quiet at night. No trains or sounds of highway traffic. Good spacing between sites. And plenty of places to ride our bikes.

Today was really cold (43 degrees). We rode the riverfront and after about 10 minutes our hands and noses were really frigid. We ducked into a rehab hospital and chatted with Sharon, the receptionist, for about 10 minutes, then ventured out again.

To get away from the colder river air we went west into Vidalia. We rode up and down the streets — amazed at the poverty, as evidenced by the number of run down and totally abandoned houses. My goodness, within only a few blocks we counted 10 or 12 dead houses, merely held up by a few stubborn boards and some crafty termites.

We rode 2 or 3 miles down the levee and had no traffic, but rocky roads. Lois got a flat. I fixed it. We were ready for the next day.

I'll try to write a little more in the future because I don't know how much future the Lord will grant me. Lois and I have had many happy years together, have raised four wonderful sons, and have seen a little of this great country of ours. I hope we can enjoy many more years together before the final sunset. We love our sons, their wives, and our fantastic 11 grandchildren. They all bring us much joy!

**Kent & sons Erik, Jared, Shane, Jay**

**All 11 Grandchildren**
Top row, left to right: Connor, Carter, Riley, Madysn
Middle row, left to right: Hannah, Tyler, Jacob, Paige
Front: Isaac, Hailey, & Noah (with arms crossed)

# 30

## *What's It Like to Be Sixty-Six?*

The short answer is: not as good as 36, but a whole lot better than 96! As to the long answer, I am in a dilemma as to which end of the body to address first? The head? The feet? Somewhere in the middle?

Oh, what's the use? I don't need to be diplomatic about something as common as age. There must be millions of people who are now sixty-six, and then think of all the folks who already have passed through this age without a wheeze or a whimper. It's not such a big deal — is it? Another thing, how a feller feels at a particular age is highly personal. Some people look like a bald tire or a sway back nag at thirty-five, because they have been ridden hard, put away wet, and slept on a bad mattress all their lives. Others at eighty or ninety look like freshly starched shirts or nervous teenagers. Yes, age is very subjective. A hard life produces hard lines and crooked joints, I guess. And an easy one? Well, you fill in the rest.

Then there comes the difference between apparent age and intrinsic age. You may be forty-five, but due to multiple ailments — most of which you caused yourself through neglect and bad choices — you look like sixty-five and feel like ninety-five. Or, physically you look like you're in fine fettle and you may be, but your mind is shot and so you don't have the mental capacity to appreciate your physical blessings. You don't know your own birth date, and you can't remember ever eating Thanksgiving turkey. But you look great, and your shape is evidence enough that you not only have never missed a Thanksgiving feast, but you haven't missed any meals in the last fifty years!

But I ramble.

Back to the point: the body at sixty-six, or, at least my body at sixty-six. Let's start at the North Pole and work our way south, painfully. My mind seems to be okay. It's as active as ever, but it takes longer to memorize the simplest of poems. I am still an active reader, but I can't remember much of what goes through my brain. I still learn new vocabulary words and I actually try to use them. Sometimes I draw strange looks when I do. Who doesn't know the meaning of quakebuttock, or dissemble, or blandish?

The years have softened me some. I am much more tolerant of contrary opinions than I used to be. Maybe I've just found better friends, those who agree with me. The last two years have been exhilarating. In retirement I have been better able to regulate my personal study time. The morning sessions from 6 to 7 have done much to both broaden and deepen my understanding of history, particularly U.S. history. These refreshing sessions have become a serious habit now and I hope to continue them for the duration of earth life.

In sum, though both my eyes have vitreous detachments, and need two types of glasses (one for close reading and one for distance), one of my ears is faulty, several teeth are crowned or round, my nose is crooked, and my hair has long ago lost its natural color (but I still have hair!), all other departments of my head seem young as ever. For this I am grateful.

**Shoulders.** They both hurt from time to time, especially if I sleep on my stomach. The right one is acquainted with cortisone and that long needle. Lately, however, it's holding its own. The left side has been serviceable for common use, except after I've spent a night of slumber on my front side. Then it screams for a few hours. Got to watch that carefully.

**From shoulders to wrists** I'm good to go, but my hands should stay at home. Carpal tunnel syndrome plagues them. I know the buzz of numb hands. I know the feeling of waking up with my hands still snoring. I know the tingle from writing too long. Nocturnal wrist braces help a great deal, but wearing them is akin to sleeping with your arms in casts. My doctor says I'll not need surgery if I wear them. My wife says wear them but never mind the back rubs. I say, wear them out — quickly — and trash them!

**The hands.** Yes. Well, left and right show strong similarities to Blanche's hands, especially the last joints. I'm talking about arthritis. Those end joints are sore and tight and swollen. My hands feel fine — if I don't use them. Well, duh! What kind of life would I have if I didn't use my hands? But let's move on.

Because this report is for general consumption, we'll skip over everything from the belly button to the knees. Gotta keep this clean. Okay, **the knees**. Ligaments near the patella are whimpering for understanding. Or maybe it's cartilage. They've had a tough life jumping and cavorting about. I get some interesting creaks and snaps from my knees. Deep Heat and knee braces help. But the knees continue to support me at the gym. And, I can still walk, and jog, but jogging is not my exercise of choice because of my feet. Now we're getting down to where the leather hits the pavement.

Bilateral axonal idiopathic peripheral neuropathy. What a mouthful. Simply put, I have nerve deterioration in both feet, and the cause is unknown, or idiopathic — that's the word for "don't know the cause." The same doc who put me in wrist shackles told me nothing would cure my neuropathy! That filled me with hope. He did prescribe the most expensive medication next to that used in rabies treatment. Lyrica is why I'm seeking another career. It's why I raided my 401-K before I retired. It's why we were forced to downgrade our choice of motels, all the way to 6. And to sprinkle tears over this pall of financial pain, I don't know if Lyrica is helping me. I know it's not helping my budget.

How bad is my neuropathy, you ask? The doc hit his tuning fork a smart blow, placed it on the big toe of my left foot, and asked, "Can you feel that?" I felt nothing, nada, zilch. He might as well have placed a cotton ball on my toe. No feeling, zero, left or right, nothing. But, he assures me that deterioration of the nerves will be slow. That's what they all say, no? But I still have strength and balance and flexion, so why cry?

Well, that's it. We've traveled my body pole to pole. What's it like being six and sixty? A lot like being six and fifty, or six and forty, or even six and thirty, I guess. It's just that while your mental or emotional game may be improving, your physical game is going to Hades in a Hummer. A handcart just doesn't indicate the proper speed of decline.

I know what you're thinking. The short answer was all you wanted. Well, I've been thinking about this for a long, long time, and a short answer, like the handcart, just doesn't do this topic justice. So, I apologize if I've told you too much. But, then again, if you're on the lighter side of sixty-six, perhaps I have given you a helpful travel guide. If you've already slipped past this milestone, you probably haven't read this far, so you don't give a rip anyway.

What's it like being sixty-six? It sure beats the whey out of the alternative.

**NOTE:** Now I am seventy-six and I just read what I wrote a decade earlier. It's really nice to be reminded of my condition ten years ago. I'm still perambulating along. What will ten more bring? (Truthfully, I'm not the least bit curious!)

# 31

## *Did You Ever?*

- Break a thorn from a rose bush, lick its base and then stick it on your nose like a mini-rhino?

- Pop a handful of wheat into your mouth and chew it into a pasty gum?

- Make a handgun from just a piece of conduit, firecracker and marble?

- Attach playing cards to the forks of your bike and let the spokes whap them in rapid succession, simulating a motorcycle?

- Leave a box of chocolates on your 12-year-old heartthrob's doorstep, knock and run because you were too chicken to face her with your gift?

- Hypnotize a frog by placing him belly up and, while holding him by the hind legs, stroking his tummy gently with a piece of straw or shaft of weed?

- Go skinny-dipping in the creek or nearby pond?

- Smash aluminum cans so that they attach to your shoes and then stomp around making loud metallic noises with them?

- Dunk for apples in a washtub at your friend's birthday party?

- Shoot ducks in the moonlight?

- Eat a dog biscuit just because you were curious about its taste?

- Have boat races in an irrigation ditch using hollowed out cucumbers as boats?

- Put a penny on a railroad track and wait for the train to come and smash it flat?

- Stomp on ice puddles in the winter all the way to school until you arrived tardy?

- Put orange peel wedges in your mouth and turn your pearly whites to orange?

- Play mumbletypeg with a jackknife and a friend, sticking the blade in the grass next to your opponents' feet?

- Play "burnout" with a baseball, throwing it as hard as you can at your opponent, attempting to burn him out of the game?

- Play "midnight basketball" where only the glow of the moon lighted the ball, your teammates, and the hoop?

- Take a wooden spring clothespin and, through clever rearranging of the three parts and a little tape, turn it into a match shooter capable of launching a burning match 10 or 15 yards hence?

- Gig for carp? (All it takes is a nice gig and a lake or river teeming with carp.)

- Think an umbrella could be used as a parachute, then try it by jumping off the roof of a shed or barn?

- Send a soup can skyward with the aid of water, a tuna can, and a firecracker?

- Blow a mailbox clean off its perch with an M-80 firecracker?

- Ride a bicycle backwards by sitting on the handlebars, belly pointed rearward?

- Write an honest-to-goodness book and have it published?

- Attend a high school reunion, long after graduation, and have a pretty classmate tell you that you were her first crush?

- Assume a fictitious name and "rubber hose" a woman at her place of employment for a bad debt owed to your sibling?

- Leave a stink bomb in the local library for the librarian to enjoy?

- Play hooky and spend the afternoon with your sister rolling down the creek bank while the gurgling water rushed by?

- Write a personal note inside a book and leave it in a motel room for a stranger to find?

- Drop kick a basketball into the hoop from twenty-five feet away?

- Launch a tire or two from a moving vehicle and then track its path from behind?

- Own a 1931 Chevrolet sedan, complete with window blinds and two spares?

- Do a random act of kindness just for the feeling of goodness that comes from doing so?

**Well, I did.**

## *Afterword – Read On!*

### RKT's 100 Great Books to Lend & Love

What are the criteria for inclusion on this list? Simple. First, no anthologies of any kind allowed (generally). Second, there is no distinction between so-called "children's literature," and "adult literature." Good literature is good literature. Next, excepting poetry, like Ogden Nash's Good Intentions, if you can honestly answer "YES" to four of the first six questions, the book is a candidate for inclusion. A "NO" answer to number seven is an automatic disqualifier. (There are more than enough excellent books with clean language to choose from.)

1. Would you read the book a second or third time? (This assumes that **a.)** the author is very good at his craft, and **b.)** that you would recommend the book to a friend.)
2. Does the book offer facts, events, places or people of historical interest and/or significance?
3. Does the book contain some morally redeeming lesson for the reader?
4. Does it evoke emotions of pity, anger, elation — make you laugh, cry or both?

5. Does it have a compelling plot — something that draws you in and keeps you?
6. Does the book have interesting, life-like characters, people you'd like to meet?
7. Is the book free of hard-core language, like the F word, or raunchy sex scenes?

***Note:*** *The books are not listed in any particular order. The book's numbered position on the list is merely for tracking and filing purposes. I have given some of the super good books an A+ or an A++ rating. Of course, that's my opinion. Finally, the list is fluid and changes with my opinion as I read more and more books, then compare and make changes as needed.*

—

### 1. The Killer Angels (1974)
Michael Shaara
*Moving acct. of Bat. of Gettysburg* **A+**

### 2. The Education of Little Tree
Forrest Carter
*Native American Bio: Excellent!*

### 3. Bury My Heart at Wounded Knee (1971)
Dee Brown
*Indian History of American West* **A+ +**

### 4. Where the Red Fern Grows (I've rd 27 x)
Wilson Rawls
*Fiction (super read!) Favorite;* **A+**

### 5. The Little World of Don Camillo (1950)
Giovanni Guareschi (translation)
*Hilarious story of Italian priest/warm*

**6. To Dance with the White Dog**
   Terry Kay
   *Fiction (Love, family), terrific;* **A+**

**7. A Thief of Time** (1988)
   Tony Hillerman
   *Leaphorn; Anasazi ruins & death!* **A+**

**8. The Professor and the Madman** (1998)
   Simon Winchester
   *Tale of murder & Oxford Dictionary*

**9. The Call of the Wild**
   Jack London
   *A dog/wolf adventure - Classic*

**10. Haunted Mesa**
   Louis L'Amour
   *Superb Sci-Fi/Anasazi Adventure*

**11. The Tracker**
   W. Jon Watkins
   *Bio of Tom Brown, Jr. —Super!*

**12. The Red Pony**
   John Steinbeck
   *Fiction—boy, colt, CA*

**13. The Way West** (Pulitzer Prize, 1950)
   A.B. Guthrie, Jr. (1949)
   *MO to Oregon, 1840s —great story!*

**14. Epitaph for a Peach** (1995)
   David Mas Masumoto
   *4 seasons on a Fresno tree farm* **A-**

**15. North to Freedom** (1963, Gyldendal Prize)
Anne Holm (Danish to Eng.)
*David escapes from prison camp*

**16. The Greatest Salesman in the World** (1968)
Og Mandino
*A blockbuster self-help book*

**17. Lassie Come-Home** (1940)
Eric Knight
*Classic story of love, poverty & will!*

**18. O Pioneers!** (1913)
Willa Cather
*Surrogate parent Alexa. Bergson* **A**

**19. The Pearl**
John Steinbeck
*People & Principles*

**20. As A Man Thinketh** (1968)
James Allen
*Inspirational Classic*

**21. The Human Comedy** (1943)
William Saroyan
*A touching fable by a gifted writer*

**22. The No. 1 Ladies' Detective Agency** (1998)
Alexander McCall Smith
*Honest, humorous, captivating!*

**23. Standing for Something** (2000)
Gordon B. Hinckley
*No-nonsense advice on 10 virtues* **A**

**24. The Shepherd of the Hills** (1907)
Harold Bell Wright
*Gentle yet compelling story of hope!*

**25. Tombstone** (1929)
Walter Noble Burns
*An Iliad of the Southwest. Well done!*

**26. The Old Man and the Sea** (1952)
Ernest Hemingway
*Man vs. giant marlin, a classic tale.*

**27. Band of Brothers** (1992) WWII 101st Airborne
Stephen E. Ambrose
*From Normandy to Eagle's Nest* **A+**

**28. The Great Train Robbery**
Michael Crichton
*Brit. train robbery of 1855; true;* **A+!**

**29. Pride & Prejudice** (1813) [First Impressions]
Jane Austen
*Excel. Classic; should read over & over!*

**30. All Creatures, Things Bright, Things Wise, & Lord God** (4 Volumes)
James Herriot
*Experience of country vet (great read!)*

**31. Common Sense** (Feb. 1776)
Thomas Paine, staymaker
*The bk that sparked independence*

**32. America** (1944)
Stephen Vincent Benet
*A reaffirmation of faith in America!*

## 33. Roll of Thunder, Hear My Cry
Mildred D. Taylor
*Awards! Black life in Miss.*

## 34. Guernsey Lit & Potato Peel Pie Society
Mary Ann Shaffer/Annie Barrows
*Unique epistolary novel of WWII*

## 35. The Year of Decision: 1846
Bernard DeVoto
*Fantastic work of history!* **A+**

## 36. Team of Rivals [Lincoln's Cabinet]
Doris Kearns Goodwin
*Political Genius of A. Lincoln* **A+**

## 37. Silas Marner
George Eliot
*Profound change in a man; great!*

## 38. All I Really Need to Know I Learned in Kindergarten
Robert Fulghum
*Philosophical Humor on life*

## 39. Jeb Stuart: The Last Cavalier (1957)
Burke Davis
*Fantastic Bio of JEB Stuart, CSA* **A+**

## 40. A Christmas Gift
Glendon Swarthout
*Wonderful rural MI farm story*

## 41. The Adventures of Tom Sawyer (1875)
Mark Twain
*Classic Boyhood Adventure -* **A+**

## 42. Profiles in Courage (1956)
John F. Kennedy
*True courage of Am. statesmen*

## 43. John Adams (2001)
David McCullough
*Very good bio; great research!!* **A**

## 44. Unbroken (2014)
Laura Hillenbrand
*Courage of Louis Zamperini* **A+**

## 45. A Fine and Pleasant Misery (+all his others)
Patrick F. McManus
*Best outdoor humor in the world!*

## 46. The Heart is a Lonely Hunter (1940)
Carson McCullers
*A story of moral isolation; GA '30s*

## 47. Anne of Green Gables (1908)
Lucy Maud Montgomery
*Anne Shirley, orphan extraordinaire!*

## 48. A Day No Pigs Would Die
Robert Newton Peck
*Biographical Fiction; very moving!* **A**

## 49. Fire of the Covenant (1999)
Gerald N. Lund
*Terrific book of Willie/Martin handcart cos.*

## 50. To Kill A Mockingbird (1960)
Harper Lee
*Pulitzer Prize , a real winner!* **A++**

## 51. Lost Men of American History (1946)
Stewart H. Holbrook
*Anthology of dozens of great men!*

## 52. David Copperfield (1850)
Charles Dickens
*"My best," says Dickens. Great!* **A+**

## 53. The Good Earth (1931) —Pulitzer winner!
Pearl S. Buck
*Classic of pre-revolutionary China*

## 54. Incident at Hawk's Hill
Allan W. Eckert
*Ben & animals survive; poignant!*

## 55. Love is Eternal (1954)
Irving Stone
*Mary Todd + Abe Lincoln* **A++!**

## 56. Good Intentions (I have 5 books by O.N.)
Ogden Nash
*Collection of Nash's verses ('37)* **A+**

## 57. The Bear (orig. The Grizzly King, 1916)
James Oliver Curwood
*Bear/man adventure story - v.g. read!*

## 58. Home to Harmony (2002)
Philip Gulley
*Small-town life with Quaker humor*

**59. Across Five Aprils** (NB honor)
Irene Hunt
*A divided family & the Civil War*

**60. John Paul Jones: Man of Action** (1927)
Phillips Russell
*Great bio of a brave admiral!* **A+**

**61. Desperate Passage** (2008)
Ethan Rarick
*Donner Party's perilous journey--* **A+**

**62. A Tree Grows in Brooklyn** (1943)
Betty Smith
*A profoundly moving & honest novel. Loved it!* **A+**

**63. Tombstone: An Iliad of the Southwest** (1927)
Walter Noble Burns
*A colorful history by a great writer!*

**64. Seabiscuit** (2001)
Laura Hillenbrand
*Spellbinding story of an unlikely champ!*

**65. All Over but the Shoutin'** (1997)
Rick Bragg (terrific writer!!)
*Life in South: poignant memoir* **A+**

**66. The Looking Glass** (1999)
Richard Paul Evans
*Old West story of love & redemption*

**67. King Solomon's Mines** (1885)
H. Rider Haggard
*Old tale of Africa which wears well!*

**68. Journey**
James A. Michener
*The Klondike Gold rush of 1897* **A**

**69. The Man Who Refused to Die**
Barry Wynne
*True acct of 64-day Pacific survival!*

**70. Papa, My Father**
Leo Buscaglia
*A tender celebration of a dad*

**71. Old Yeller**
Fred Gipson
*Classic dog tale which hits the heart*

**72. A River Runs Through It**
Norman MacLean
*Frontier MT-Pulit. Prize nominee*

**73. Never Cry Wolf**
Farley Mowat
*True-life among Arctic wolves!* **A+**

**74. The Case of the Perjured Parrot** (1939)
Erle Stanley Gardner
*A great murder mystery by a pro.*

**75. Gone with the Wind** (1936)
Margaret Mitchell
*Tragic CW story of Scarlett O'Hara et al* **A+**

**76. The Human Comedy** (1943)
William Saroyan
*A touching fable by a gifted writer*

**77. The Friendly Persuasion** (1945)
  Jessamyn West
  *Jess/Eliza Birdwell, Irish Quakers* **A+**

**78. Too Many Cooks** (1938)
  Rex Stout
  *A Nero Wolfe/Archie Goodwin tale*

**79. QB** (My Life Behind the Spiral)
  Steve Young & Jeff Benedict
  *A look into this QB's heart & soul* **A++**

**80. Shoeless Joe**
  W.P. Kinsella
  *Source story for Field of Dreams* **A+**

**81. Daisy Fay and the Miracle Man**
  Fannie Flagg
  *Wonderfully-funny, crisp novel* **A**

**82. Happy Homes & the Hearts that Make Them**
  Samuel Smiles
  *See Chapter 21 in this volume.*

**83. Laughing Boy** (Pul. Prize, 1930)
  Oliver La Farge (1929)
  *A threatened love, Navajo style*

**84. The Long Walk** (1960) [true!]
  Slavomir Rawicz
  *Escape from Siberia, 1939;* **A++*!***

**85. Home Country** (1947)
  Ernie Pyle
  *Selected E.P. articles over 5 years* **A+**

**86. The Red Badge of Courage** (1895)
Stephen Crane
*Episode of the Am. Civil War (classic)*

**87. A Summons to Memphis** (1986)
Peter Taylor
*Pu Prize; Fa/Son reconciliation* **A+**

**88. Last of the Breed**
Louis L'Amour
*Epic novel of escape from Russia!* **A**

**89. The Lame, The Halt, and the Blind** (1932)
Howard W. Haggard, M.D.
*Vital Role of medicine in history* **A+**

**90. Lake Wobegon Days** (1985)
Garrison Keillor
*Rich stories by a gifted humorist*

**91. The End of The Road** (1989)
Tom Bodett
*Bodettish warmth & humor—great!*

**92. The Robe** (1942)
Lloyd C. Douglas
*The power of Christ's robe.* **A+**

**93. The Murder Trial of Judge Peel** (1962)
Jim Bishop
*True acct. of murder in Florida, 1955*

**94. The Nameless Breed** (1960)
Will C. Brown (WWA Spur Award)
Texas, 1844 great western

**95. The Pastures of Heaven** (1932)
   John Steinbeck
   *Vignettes of families in CA valley*

**96. The Yearling** (1938, Pulitzer for fiction)
   Marjorie Kinnan Rawlings
   *Jody Baxter's coming of age!* **A+**

**97. The Star-Gazer** (Bio of Galileo, 1939)
   Zsolt De Harsanyi
   *Excellent bio; Galileo vs. Church* **A++**

**98. Crooked House** (1949)
   Agatha Christie
   *Vintage mystery by the master.* **A**

**99. Vengeance Trail** (1931)
   Max Brand [Fred Faust]
   *Wonderful action-packed tale.* **A++**

**100. A Christmas Carol** (1843)
   Charles Dickens
   *Classic tale of Scrooge —* **A+**

## The Waiting List

The following books are all terrific books. Some have received high praise by experts and/or organizations of distinguished repute. However, they don't quite measure up to my **100 Great Books** standards, and since this is my list, I get to decide. I have included them here sort of as a list of "Second Place" winners. I may change my mind at some future date and bump an elite "100" in favor of one of these also rans.

- **The Man Who Killed the Deer** (1941)
  Frank Waters
  *American Indian life/insightful*

- **Hanging Woman Creek**
  Louis L'Amour
  *Who can handle this assignment?*

- **My Gal Sunday** (1996)
  Mary Higgins Clark
  *4 mystery stories, clean and tense!*

- **The Blue Flower** (1902)
  Henry Van Dyke
  *9 short stories with religious tone*

- **The 13 Clocks** (1 of only 3 he wrote for kids)
  James Thurber
  *Parable/fairy tale/poem w/ illus.*

- **Grant & Sherman** (2005)
    Charles Bracelen Flood
    *A fantastic bk about a friendship that won the Civil War. Truly* **A+**

- **America**
    Modern Library Anthology All about America—song and word
    *(A deeply moving book, but it's an anthology. It will likely wait forever, but definitely worth reading.)*

- **My Posse Don't Do Homework**
    LouAnne Johnson
    *Ex-Marine's 1st Yr teaching High School*

- **When the Mountain Fell** (1947)
    Charles Ferdinand Ramuz
    *Beautiful, moving love story*

- **In Cold Blood**
    Truman Capote
    *Powerful doc. of an American crime*

- **Papa Married a Mormon**
    John Fitzgerald

*Jay, Shane, Lois, Jared, & Erik — May, 2020*

*With Granddaughter Hailey, 2009*

*With Granddaughter Paige, 2007*

*Grandpa with twins Carter & Riley — 2003*

# *About the Author*

Kent Tipton, the fifth of five children, was born and raised in rural Utah. His parents were not writers, far from it. His mother was an energetic, top-flight waitress and cashier, and his father was a very hard-working heavy equipment mechanic. Tipton inherited his mother's sense of humor and his father's work ethic.

He served two years in the army, and two and one-half years as a missionary for The Church of Jesus Christ of Latter-day Saints on the island of Taiwan. There he learned to speak Chinese, and he acquired a deep respect for the Asian culture. When he returned home, he enrolled at Brigham Young University. While in a Zoology class, he met a beautiful blonde named Lois. He didn't earn a very high grade in the class, but he gained a terrific wife. A few years later he graduated with a double major: 1) Chinese Language and 2) Asian Studies. Lois graduated with a major in Elementary Education.

His first job offer out of college was from the CIA. He completed all phases of its rigorous interview process, including a polygraph test. Because of that test (there's another story here), Tipton swears by the effectiveness of the polygraph machine. "Don't even think about lying," he says. When the offer came through, Kent thought long and hard about what life in the CIA might be like. It was tempting, but in the end, he and Lois declined the offer, and he switched career paths.

Tipton began teaching a class of fourth-grade students, cautiously described by the principal as "a keg of dynamite," in St. Louis, MO. After that very trying but fulfilling year, he moved to California, obtained an advanced degree, and worked in the schools for twenty-four more years. Along the way he began recording humorous, odd, or outlandish events. Such anecdotes that occurred in the public schools became the basis of his book ***Pencil Shavings (2018).*** This volume proved the old adage: "Truth is stranger than fiction."

His first published book, ***A Different Kind of Mom***, is a tribute to his mother and her rich sense of humor. He wrote it shortly after her death on Christmas Eve of 1998. Other titles followed, all seasoned with droll humor Tipton is noted for. ***Kid Posse & the Phantom Robber*** won "Best Fiction for Young Adults" award from Mayhaven Publishing in Chicago in 2002. ***Menopausal Mama & Metamucil Man*** (2017) celebrates 50 years of married life for the author and his wife, richly salted with Tipton humor. ***Kid Posse and the Cave of Death*** (2018) picks up where ***Phantom Robber*** ends, featuring the same colorful gang of six. ***South of Trouble*** (2018) is a very lively and brutally candid account of the author's early life, featuring industrial strength pastimes of the fifties. It overflows with edgy pranks, raw danger, outlandish episodes with cars, buddies and, of course, more clean Tipton humor. A third Kid Posse book came in 2019, ***Kid Posse and the Fantastic Ice Blitzer,*** a book noted for its high-octane adventure and featuring the familiar cast of young posse members. ***The Journal*** was released in late 2019. It is a stand-alone story of a troubled boy who is struggling to find his place in his family. Finally, ***Indelible Memories of Yesteryears,*** an autobiographical memoir, and ***Eight Days of Wistful Journeys***, were released in 2020 — with one additional volume from the author expected in 2021.

## Indelible Memories of Yesteryears

Sample a bit of Tipton. Just go to **Amazon.com** and check for yourself. All of his books are there on display.

---

# Writer wins Mayhaven Award

BY GARY LINEHAN

Jamestown School teacher R. Kent Tipton has published his third book and earned a literary prize in the process.

The book, an adventure story titled "Kid Posse and the Phantom Robber," has been more than 10 years in the making, Tipton said.

After years of writing and rewriting — "most of the stories went through about 15 drafts," he said — Tipton entered his story in a contest sponsored by Mayhaven Publishing in Illinois.

"Months went by and I thought nothing of it," he said. "Then I received a phone call — wonder of wonders, I won!"

Among other honors, the 2002 Mayhaven Award for Fiction included publication of the book.

Originally aimed at middle school readers, the book also is hitting a nostalgia nerve in adults. "Most of my sales are to adults," he said.

In "Kid Posse and the Phantom Robber," Tipton weaves two stories a half-century apart. Based on an actual bank robbery of 1898 in

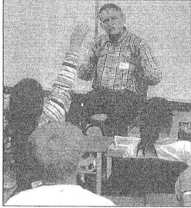

Union Democrat photo by Amy Alonzo
AUTHOR R. Kent Tipton answers questions from his readers.

Springville, Utah, the book could be classified as historical fiction. But it is also a glimpse of the author's childhood, as many of the episodes are based on true-life experiences in the same town.

"Some things did happen, some didn't, that's why it's fiction," Tipton said. "There is still $600 missing from that bank robbery. That's the truth."

The 239-page book tells of six boys chasing a dream to build a boat in the 1950s. If only they had sufficient money to buy materials. If only summers lasted 12 months instead of three. If only they could stay on track. If only they could agree on matters.

On the non-fiction side, the author's great-grandfather, Joseph William Allan, actually was the member of the posse that exchanged gunfire with "Gunplay Maxwell" and his partner, Porter, the two bandits who robbed the bank.

In fact, Allan is the one who lost half his leg to the shootout, and actually shot and killed Porter.

The book received rave reviews from a group of sixth grade students who read the book as a class project at Copperopolis School.

"Reading is my favorite subject and this is one of the best books I've ever read," said Grace Warner. "I really, really enjoyed it and I hope he writes more."

Breanna Roque agreed. "I liked it because it was interesting and had a lot of funny facts," she said. "I liked the part where (Bungy) jumped off a tree. It sounds like something a boy would do."

Robert Danner described the book as "Awesome — I loved it because it was a mystery and he described it so well you could see it in your mind. Most of the time it was non-stop laughing."

Tipton said a "Kid Posse" sequel is already written and being considered by his publisher.

"Kid Posse and the Phantom Robber" sells for $14.95. It is available at Mountain Bookshop in The Junction shopping center, Camacho's Taqueria in Sonora or by mail (add $1.50 postage) from Madrone Books, 11836 Campo Seco Road, Sonora 95370.

Tipton was born and raised in Springville, Utah, a town of about 4,000 south of Provo. He began teaching in 1967 in St. Louis and has been at Jamestown School for about 10 years.

He and his wife, Lois, a teacher at Copperopolis School, have four grown sons, all graduates of Sonora High School.

Tipton previous wrote "A Different Kind of Mom," a biographical tribute to his mother, and "In Quotes We Trust," co-authored with his wife as a reference guide for teachers.

# *Richard Kent Tipton*

## September 20, 1942 – May 11, 2020

The world has lost a truly great husband, father, teacher, author, and patriot. R. Kent Tipton passed peacefully in his Sonora, California home surrounded by loving family on May 11, 2020. During his 77 years, Kent led a life filled with laughter, service, sacrifice, creativity, leadership, a thirst for knowledge and, above all, an unwavering commitment to his beloved wife, his family, and service to God.

The youngest of 5 siblings, Kent Tipton was born in Springville, Utah on September 20, 1942 to Blanche and Norman Tipton. While his mother added the additional name of 'Richard' during his early childhood, the name Kent was how most knew him.

Kent spent his youth pursuing creative adventures with his friends - whether it be building a boat to chart the waters of a local pond or competing in 'tire rolling' contests, his ideas for fun seemed boundless. Kent graduated from Springville High School in 1960 and then served his country from 1960-62 as a member of the Army National Guard — where he was called to active duty during the Berlin Crisis.

In 1962 Kent was called to serve a mission for the Church of Jesus Christ of Latter-Day Saints, spending

30 months in the Taiwan Taipei mission. Throughout this calling, Kent immersed himself in his work, falling in love with the Taiwanese people and culture. He dedicated himself to his teachings and the language, learning to not only speak fluent Mandarin, but also to write it.

Kent's mission experience led him to dedicate his collegiate studies in the pursuit of a double major in both Chinese Language and Asian Studies at Brigham Young University. One of Kent's senior projects included translating an entire book from Mandarin to English. While at BYU, he met the love of his life, Lois Karen Bonham. The two were sealed in the Salt Lake Temple on September 1, 1967 and, shortly thereafter, both graduated from the college.

The newlyweds soon moved to California so Kent could pursue graduate school, completing his Master's in Education from CSU Bakersfield in 1974. As the couple grew their family, Kent worked in a variety of teaching and administrative roles, until leaving education to lead an international publishing and financial advisory firm in 1978, eventually taking on the role of President there. During this time, Kent was able to share his love for the Chinese culture with Lois during a business trip to Mainland China, where he also served as translator and tour guide.

Kent's entrepreneurial spirit led him to start his own successful company in 1987. Eventually, Kent's love for education returned him to classrooms in 1993, ultimately completing his career as Principal of Jamestown Elementary in 2006.

Throughout his life, Kent also dedicated himself to tireless service in his church and community. He was a constant participant in the Boy Scouts of America program, leading a multitude of activities in support of local youth with his can-do attitude toward personal growth and life skills. Kent was also called to serve in a variety of Church capacities, including that of Bishop of the Sonora First Ward in 2014. He gave each and every assignment the best of his time and talent, bringing a warm smile and welcoming ear to all those he served.

Kent's athletic pursuits in his youth, coupled with his leadership skills, enabled him to coach each one of his four sons in a variety of organized sports, including soccer, football, basketball, and baseball. Throughout his life both he and Lois found great pleasure in cheering on their alma mater in all collegiate sporting events.

In addition to all of his life's pursuits, Kent was also an accomplished writer. He published more than 10 fiction and non-fiction books. Kent's writing won him the Mayhaven Award for Children's Fiction for the first novel in his 'Kid Posse' series. His most recent fictional work, 'The Journal', was published August 5, 2019.

In retirement, Kent and Lois have been able to enjoy extensive travel together throughout the United States, exploring points of interest and history in 30 states. He also took incredible pride in home improvement efforts and a variety of woodworking projects - most of which he gave away as gifts to friends and family.

Kent will be remembered by the thousands of people he has touched — through his church service, his decades in education and private business, his written works, and the extensive family he leaves behind — for his sense of humor, intelligence, leadership, can-do attitude, and creativity. However, he will be remembered most of all for the love he will always have for his wife, his family, and his God.

His brother Jay, mother Blanche, and father Norman predeceased Kent. He is survived by his wife Lois, brothers Gary and Dean, sister Marjorie, sons

Jared, Erik, Shane, Jay, daughters-in-law Dusti, Keri, Jenny, and his eleven grandchildren: Madysn, Connor, Riley, Carter, Tyler, Jacob, Hannah, Paige, Isaac, Hailey, and Noah.

A private family memorial service was held on Saturday, May 16.

*May 16, 2020 — entire R. Kent Tipton family*

Made in the USA
Monee, IL
10 November 2020

47081159R00128